SELECTED POEMS

Günter Grass was born in Danzig (now Gdansk) in 1927.
He is the author of *The Tin Drum*, *Cat and Mouse*, *Dog Years*,
The Flounder and *The Rat*, among other novels, as well as plays
and political writings.

Michael Hamburger was born in Berlin in 1924.
A distinguished poet in his own right, he has also won
many prizes for his translations of German poetry.

Günter Grass   SELECTED POEMS

translated by Michael Hamburger

faber and faber

First published in 1999
by Faber and Faber Limited
3 Queen Square London WC1N 3AU

Photoset by Wilmaset Ltd, Wirral
Printed in England by MacKays of Chatham plc, Chatham, Kent

A CIP record for this book
is available from the British Library

ISBN 0–571–19518–0

10 9 8 7 6 5 4 3 2 1

Contents

Translator's Preface, ix

from *Die Vorzüge der Windhühner* (1956)

Geöffneter Schrank
    Open Wardrobe, 2
Polnische Fahne
    Flag of Poland, 4
Prophetenkost
    Prophets' Fare, 6
Tierschutz
    Prevention of Cruelty to Animals, 8
Misslungener Überfall
    Unsuccessful Raid, 10
Familiär
    Family Matters, 12

from *Gleisdreieck* (1960)

Kinderlied
    Nursery Rhyme, 14
Wandlung
    Transformation, 16
Klappstühle
    Folding Chairs, 18
Im Ei
    In the Egg, 20
Ausverkauf
    Sale, 24

Die Vogelscheuchen
      The Scarecrows, 26
Kleine Aufforderung zum grossen Mundaufmachen –
oder der Wasserspeier spricht
      Little Address Calling for a Great Opening of Mouths –
      or the Gargoyle Speaks, 30
Köche und Löffel
      Chefs and Spoons, 32
Zauberei mit den Bräuten Christi
      Magical Exercise with the Brides of Christ, 36
Die Seeschlacht
      The Sea Battle, 42
Aus dem Alltag der Puppe Nana
      From the Daily Life of the Doll Nana, 44
Mein Radiergummi
      My Eraser, 52
Die Grosse Trümmerfrau Spricht
      The Great Rubblewoman Speaks, 58
Ehe
      Marriage, 68
Plötzliche Angst
      Sudden Fright, 72
König Lear
      King Lear, 74
Schlaflos
      Sleepless, 76
Liebe
      Love, 78
Hymne
      Hymn, 80
Schreiben
      Writing, 82

Die Peitsche
    The Whip, 86
Das Dampfkessel-Effekt
    The Steam Boiler Effect, 88
In Ohnmacht gefallen
    Powerless, with a Guitar, 90
Irgendwas machen
    Do Something, 92
Die Schweinekopfsülze
    The Jellied Pig's Head, 102

from *Liebe Geprüft* (1974)

Liebe Geprüft
    Love Tested, 110
Dein Ohr
    Your Ear, 113

from *Der Butt/The Flounder* (1977)

Gestillt
    Comforted, 114
Wie Ich mich sehe
    How I See Myself, 116

Scattered Poems

Sargnägel
    Coffin Nails, 118
Müll unser
    Our Litter Which, 120

Abschied nehmen
    Leavetaking, 122

Novemberland

Das Unsre
    What's Ours, 130
Novemberland
    Novemberland, 132
Späte Sonnenblumen
    Late Sunflowers, 134
Allerseelen
    All Souls, 136
Sturmwarnung
    Gale Warning, 138
Vorm ersten Advent
    Before the First Sunday in Advent, 141
Ausser Plan
    Unplanned, 142
Andauernder Regen
    Persistent Rain, 144
Die Festung Wächst
    The Fortress Grows, 146
Entlaubt
    Defoliated, 148
Nach kurzer Krankheit
    After Brief Illness, 150
Bei klarer Sicht
    In Clear Perspective, 152
Wer kommt?
    Who's Coming? 154

Translator's Preface

Günter Grass's first book was a collection of poems, with graphics of his own. Then came the large-scale fantastic and satirical novels, *The Tin Drum* and *Dog Years*, to which he owes most of his international readership and fame. Prolific as he has remained as a novelist, he has never ceased to return to his first literary medium, more often than not in conjunction with his even earlier skills as a draughtsman, etcher and watercolourist, for which he had been trained at art school after employment as a stone-carver. Books of poems and limited editions of poems with related graphics or paintings have continued to appear up to the volume *Fundsachen für Nichtleser* (Found Things for Non-Readers), published for his seventieth birthday in 1997. Significantly, too, several of his later novels include poems that are integral parts of their imaginative and thematic structure, yet remarkable enough out of context to be represented in the present selection.

This selection draws on all his poems published since the first book of 1956, up to, but not including, his most recent book of 1997, in which the texts are inseparable from the watercolours that go with them, as the title indicates. Some of the poems chosen here – by Christopher Reid, Poetry Editor at Faber – replace earlier selections published by Secker & Warburg and by Penguin Books, others complement these with later work published only in limited editions or in the American selection *Novemberland* of 1996.

From the first, and in all his media, it has been Günter Grass's distinction to strike a peculiar balance between the usually irreconcilable extremes of personal, almost obsessive idiosyncrasy on the one hand, and of social conscience and social vision on the other. When he began to write, these opposing extremes, in German literature, were typified by two older writers who died in 1956, Gottfried Benn and Bertolt Brecht. Grass's awareness of the division and his determination to overcome it can be traced back to his earliest prose pieces, published as 'Der Inhalt as Widerstand' (Content as Resistance). Later, he characterized his own function as that of 'the court fool, in the absence of Courts'. He had realized that the ideological 'commitment' almost obligatory for West German writers in the sixties and seventies was incompatible with the imaginative freedom he had always needed for his work, though not with the ethical concerns and responsibility equally essential to it. In fact the absence of a Court in West Germany did not preclude the privilege once accorded to court fools – that of telling disagreeable truths. As a citizen, not as an artist, Grass could even commit himself for a time to a political party, the Social Democrats, electioneering for it with impassioned speeches. But when the passion and the vision ceased to tally with party policies, Grass could remain a controversial political figure, because for the German press and media, unlike the British, the opinions and stances of eminent writers belong to the public realm.

Grass's beginnings as a poet, prose writer, dramatist and visual artist are closer to the Expressionist freedoms of Gottfried Benn (and of Grass's 'teacher', as he called him, Alfred Döblin), even of Surrealism and Dadaism, than to the 'committed' muse whom Grass described as 'grey, mistrustful and totally dreamless, a meticulous housewife' in one of those early prose pieces, though his implicit ethical and social responsibilities were never in abeyance. At the same time Grass had found a special affinity to earlier literary traditions, to the German picaresque novel of the sixteenth century, the much older one of the fairy tale and, in poetry, to the baroque mode akin to 'metaphysical verse' in English. The last is most evident in his sonnet sequence 'Novemberland', at once the most topical of his later sequences and the most indebted to baroque prosody and conceits. In his later fiction, too, Grass's exuberant and grotesque invention has tended to be curbed by the demands of the 'grey', more sober muse – to the point of a seeming self-identification with the Prussian novelist Fontane's no-nonsense naturalism in the most recent novel – but for a special polemical purpose only, and not at the expense of the court fool's necessary freedom.

Yet Grass's gusto and energy are immediately recognizable as his, and his alone, in his poems of any period – just as his sensuous response to visible, tangible and tastable things is immediately recognizable in the most bizarrely subliminal or fantastic of his graphic works, always executed with a master's grasp of minute detail. Yet another of his accomplishments and delights, cookery, has entered into the texture of his verse, prose and visual art. Perhaps because innocence and experiences have blended so happily and distinctly in everything he has done, so that children's games and nursery rhymes could serve him to damn the joylessness and repressiveness of adult bureaucracy – 'Kinderlied' is Grass's own favourite among his poems – one feels that all his diverse and wide-ranging skills have flowed from a single source.

M.H.
February 1998

Selected Poems

Geöffneter Schrank

Unten stehen die Schuhe.
Sie fürchten sich vor einem Käfer
auf dem Hinweg,
vor einem Pfennig auf dem Rückweg,
vor Käfer und Pfennig die sie treten könnten
bis es sich einprägt.
Oben ist die Heimat der Hüte.
Behüte, hüte dich, behutsam.
Unglaubliche Federn,
wie hieß der Vogel,
wohin rollte sein Blick
als er einsah, daß er zu bunt geraten?
Die weißen Kugeln, die in den Taschen schlafen,
träumen von Motten.
Hier fehlt ein Knopf,
im Gürtel ermüdet die Schlange.
Schmerzliche Seide,
Astern und andere feuergefährliche Blumen,
der Herbst, der zum Kleid wird,
jeden Sonntag mit Fleisch und dem Salz
gefälteter Wäsche gefüllt.
Bevor der Schrank schweigt, Holz wird,
ein entfernter Verwandter der Kiefer, –
wer wird den Mantel tragen
wenn du einmal tot bist?
Seinen Arm im Ärmel bewegen,
zuvorkommend jeder Bewegung?
Wer wird den Kragen hochschlagen,
vor den Bildern stehen bleiben
und alleine sein unter der windigen Glocke?

[2]

Open Wardrobe

The shoes are at the bottom.
They are afraid of a beetle
on the way out,
of a penny on the way back,
of a beetle and a penny on which they might tread
till it impresses itself.
At the top is the home of the headgear.
Take heed, be wary, not headstrong.
Incredible feathers,
what was the bird called,
where did its eyes roll
when it knew that its wings were too gaudy?
The white balls asleep in the pockets
dream of moths.
Here a button is missing,
in this belt the snake grows weary.
Doleful silk,
asters and other inflammable flowers,
autumn becoming a dress.
Every Sunday filled with flesh
and the salt of creased linen.
Before the wardrobe falls silent, turns into wood,
a distant relation of pine trees –
who will wear the coat
one day when you're dead?
Who move his arm in the sleeve,
anticipate every movement?
Who will turn up the collar,
stop in front of the pictures
and be alone under the windy cloche?

Viel Kirschen die aus diesem Blut
im Aufbegehren deutlich werden,
das Bett zum roten Inlett überreden.

Der erste Frost zählt Rüben, blinde Teiche,
Kartoffelfeuer überm Horizont,
auch Männer halb im Rauch verwickelt.

Die Tage schrumpfen, Äpel auf dem Schrank,
die Freiheit fror, jetzt brennt sie in den Öfen,
kocht Kindern Brei und malt die Knöchel rot.

Im Schnee der Kopftücher beim Fest,
Pilsudskis Herz, des Pferdes fünfter Huf,
schlug an die Scheune, bis der Starost kam.

Die Fahne blutet musterlos,
so kam der Winter, wird der Schritt
hinter den Wölfen Warschau finden.

Flag of Poland

Plenty of cherries that from this blood
in wishing's upsurge become clear,
persuade the bed to be an inlet, red.

First frost counts turnips, ponds gone blind,
potato fires above the horizon
and men half tangled in the smoke.

The days are shrinking, apples on the cupboard,
liberty froze, now it burns in the stoves,
cooks porridge for children and paints ankles red.

In the snow of headshawls at the fête
Pilsudski's heart, the fifth hoof of the horse,
knocked on the barn till the Starosty came.

The flag is bleeding patternless,
so winter came, the plodding steps
behind the wolves will find Warsaw.

Prophetenkost

Als Heuschrecken unsere Stadt besetzten,
keine Milch mehr ins Haus kam, die Zeitung erstickte,
öffnete man die Kerker, gab die Propheten frei.
Nun zogen sie durch die Straßen, 3800 Propheten.
Ungestraft durften sie reden, sich reichlich nähren
von jenem springenden, grauen Belag, den wir die Plage
    nannten.
Wer hätte es anders erwartet. –

Bald kam uns wieder die Milch, die Zeitung atmete auf,
Propheten füllten die Kerker.

Prophets' Fare

When locusts occupied our city
no more milk reached our houses, the newspaper choked,
the prison cells were opened, the prophets set free.
Now they moved through the streets in procession, 3,800
    prophets.
They could speak with impunity, and eat their fill
of that jumping, grey surface cover
that we called the plague.
Who would have expected any other outcome. –

Soon the milk came back to us, the newspaper found its
    breath,
prophets filled the prison cells.

Tierschutz

Das Klavier in den Zoo.
Schnell, bringt das Zebra in die gute Stube.
Seid freundlich mit ihm,
es kommt aus Bechstein.
Noten frißt es
und unsere süßen Ohren.

Prevention of Cruelty to Animals

The piano into the zoo.
Quick, get the zebra into the best room.
Be kind to it,
it comes from Bechstein.
Scores are its fodder,
and our sweet ears.

Am Mittwoch.
Jeder wußte wieviele Treppen hinauf,
den Druck auf den Knopf,
die zweite Tür links.
Sie stürmten die Kasse.
Es war aber Sonntag
und das Geld in der Kirche.

Unsuccessful Raid

On Wednesday.
Everyone knew how many steps,
which bell to ring,
the second door on the left.
They smashed the till.
But it was Sunday
and the cash was at church.

Familiär

In unserem Museum, – wir besuchen es jeden Sonntag, –
hat man eine neue Abteilung eröffnet.
Unsere abgetriebenen Kinder, blasse, ernsthafte Embryos,
sitzen dort in schlichten Gläsern
und sorgen sich um die Zukunft ihrer Eltern.

Family Matters

In our museum – we always go there on Sundays –
they have opened a new department.
Our aborted children, pale, serious embryos,
sit there in plain glass jars
and worry about their parents' future.

Kinderlied

Wer lacht hier, hat gelacht?
Hier hat sich's ausgelacht.
Wer hier lacht, macht Verdacht,
daß er aus Gründen lacht.

Wer weint hier, hat geweint?
Hier wird nicht mehr geweint.
Wer hier weint, der auch meint,
daß er aus Gründen weint.

Wer spricht hier, spricht und schweigt?
Wer schweigt, wird angezeigt.
Wer hier spricht, hat verschwiegen,
wo seine Gründe liegen.

Wer spielt hier, spielt im Sand?
Wer spielt, muß an die Wand,
hat sich beim Spiel die Hand
gründlich verspielt, verbrannt.

Wer stirbt hier, ist gestorben?
Wer stirbt, ist abgeworben.
Wer hier stirbt, unverdorben
ist ohne Grund verstorben.

Nursery Rhyme

Who laughs here, who has laughed?
Here we have ceased to laugh.
To laugh here now is treason.
The laugher has a reason.

Who weeps here, who has wept?
Here weeping is inept.
To weep here now means too
a reason so to do.

Who speaks here or keeps mum?
Here we denounce the dumb.
To speak here is to hide
deep reasons kept inside.

Who plays here, in the sand?
Against the wall we stand
players whose games are banned.
They've lost, thrown in their hand.

Who dies here, dares to die?
'Defector!' here we cry.
To die here, without stain,
is to have died in vain.

Wandlung

Plötzlich waren die Kirschen da,
obgleich ich vergessen hatte,
daß es Kirschen gibt
und verkünden ließ: Noch nie gab es Kirschen –
waren sie da, plötzlich und teuer.

Pflaumen fielen und trafen mich.
Doch wer da denkt,
ich wandelte mich,
weil etwas fiel und mich traf,
wurde noch nie von fallenden Pflaumen getroffen.

Erst als man Nüsse in meine Schuhe schüttete
und ich laufen mußte,
weil die Kinder die Kerne wollten,
schrie ich nach Kirschen, wollt ich von Pflaumen
getroffen werden – und wandelte mich ein wenig.

Transformation

Suddenly the cherries were there
although I had forgotten
that cherries exist
and caused to be proclaimed: There never have been cherries –
they were there, suddenly and dear.

Plums fell and hit me;
but whoever thinks
that I was transformed
because something fell and hit me
has never been hit by falling plums.

Only when they poured nuts into my shoes
and I had to walk
because the children wanted the kernels
I cried out for cherries, wanted plums
to hit me – and was transformed a little.

Klappstühle

Wie traurig sind diese Veränderungen.
Die Leute schrauben ihre Namenschilder ab,
nehmen den Topf mit dem Rotkohl,
wärmen ihn auf, anderen Ortes.

Was sind das für Möbel,
die für den Aufbruch werben?
Die Leute nehmen ihre Klappstühle
und wandern aus.

Mit Heimweh und Brechreiz beladene Schiffe
tragen patentierte Sitzgelegenheiten
und patentlose Besitzer
hin und her.

Auf beiden Seiten des großen Wassers
stehen nun Klappstühle;
wie traurig sind diese Veränderungen.

Folding Chairs

How sad these changes are.
People unscrew the nameplates from the doors,
take the saucepan of cabbage
and heat it up again, in a different place.

What sort of furniture is this
that advertises departure?
People take up their folding chairs
and emigrate.

Ships laden with homesickness and the urge to vomit
carry patented seating contraptions
and their unpatented owners
to and fro.

Now on both sides of the great ocean
there are folding chairs;
how sad these changes are.

Im Ei

Wir leben im Ei.
Die Innenseite der Schale
haben wir mit unanständigen Zeichnungen
und den Vornamen unserer Feinde bekritzelt.
Wir werden gebrütet.

Wer uns auch brütet,
unseren Bleistift brütet er mit.
Ausgeschlüpft eines Tages,
werden wir uns sofort
ein Bildnis des Brütenden machen.

Wir nehmen an, daß wir gebrütet werden.
Wir stellen uns ein gutmütiges Geflügel vor
und schreiben Schulaufsätze
über Farbe und Rasse
der uns brütenden Henne.

Wann schlüpfen wir aus?
Unsere Propheten im Ei
streiten sich für mittelmäßige Bezahlung
über die Dauer der Brutzeit.
Sie nehmen einen Tag X an.

Aus Langeweile und echtem Bedürfnis
haben wir Brutkästen erfunden.
Wir sorgen uns sehr um unseren Nachwuchs im Ei.
Gerne würden wir jener, die über uns wacht
unser Patent empfehlen.

In the Egg

We live in the egg.
We have covered the inside wall
of the shell with dirty drawings
and the Christian names of our enemies.
We are being hatched.

Whoever is hatching us
is hatching our pencils as well.
Set free from the egg one day
at once we shall make an image
of whoever is hatching us.

We assume that we're being hatched.
We imagine some good-natured fowl
and write school essays
about the colour and breed
of the hen that is hatching us.

When shall we break the shell?
Our prophets inside the egg
for a middling salary argue
about the period of incubation.
They posit a day called X.

Out of boredom and genuine need
we have invented incubators.
We are much concerned about our offspring inside the egg.
We should be glad to recommend our patent
to her who looks after us.

Wir aber haben ein Dach überm Kopf.
Senile Küken,
Embryos mit Sprachkenntnissen
reden den ganzen Tag
und besprechen noch ihre Träume.

But we have a roof over our heads.
Senile chicks,
polyglot embryos
chatter all day
and even discuss their dreams.

Ausverkauf

Ich habe alles verkauft.
Die Leute stiegen vier Treppen hoch,
klingelten zweimal, atemlos
und zahlten mir auf den Fußboden,
weil der Tisch schon verkauft war.

Während ich alles verkaufte,
enteigneten sie fünf oder sechs Straßen weiter
die besitzanzeigenden Fürwörter
und sägten den kleinen harmlosen Männern
den Schatten ab, den privaten.

Ich habe alles verkauft.
Bei mir ist nichts mehr zu holen.
Selbst meinen letzten winzigsten Genitiv,
den ich von früher her anhänglich aufbewahrte,
habe ich günstig verkaufen können.

Alles habe ich verkauft.
Den Stühlen machte ich Beine,
dem Schrank sprach ich das Recht ab,
die Betten stellte ich bloß –
ich legte mich wunschlos daneben.

Am Ende war alles verkauft.
Die Hemden kragen- und hoffnungslos,
die Hosen wußten zuviel,
einem rohen blutjungen Kotelett
schenkte ich meine Bratpfanne

und gleichfalls mein restliches Salz.

[24]

Sale

I've sold out, all I owned, the lot.
Four flights of stairs they came up,
rang the bell twice, out of breath,
and paid down their cash on the floor,
since the table too had been sold.

While I was selling it all,
five or six streets from here they expropriated
all the possessive pronouns
and sawed off the private shadows
of little innocuous men.

I've sold out, all I owned, the lot.
There's no more to be had from me.
Even my last and tiniest genitive,
a keepsake long treasured devoutly,
fetched a good price in the end.

All I owned is sold now, the lot.
My old chairs – I sent them packing.
The wardrobe – I gave it the sack.
The beds – I stripped them, exposed them
and lay down beside them, abstemious.

In the end all I'd owned had been sold.
The shirts were collarless, hopeless,
the trousers by now knew too much;
to a raw and blushing young cutlet
I made a gift of my frying-pan

and all that was left of my salt.

[25]

Die Vogelscheuchen

Ich weiß nicht, ob man Erde kaufen kann,
ob es genügt, wenn man vier Pfähle,
mit etwas Rost dazwischen und Gestrüpp,
im Sand verscharrt und Garten dazu sagt.

Ich weiß nicht, was die Stare denken.
Sie flattern manchmal auf, zerstäuben,
besprenkeln meinen Nachmittag,
tun so, als könnte man sie scheuchen,
als seien Vogelscheuchen Vogelscheuchen
und Luftgewehre hinter den Gardinen
und Katzen in der Bohnensaat.

Ich weiß nicht, was die alten Jacken
und Hosentaschen von uns wissen.
Ich weiß nicht, was in Hüten brütet,
welchen Gedanken was entschlüpft
und flügge wird und läßt sich nicht verscheuchen;
von Vogelscheuchen werden wir behütet.

Sind Vogelscheuchen Säugetiere?
Es sieht so aus, als ob sie sich vermehren,
indem sie nachts die Hüte tauschen:
schon stehn in meinem Garten drei,
verneigen sich und winken höflich
und drehen sich und zwinkern mit der Sonne
und reden, reden zum Salat.

Ich weiß nicht, ob mein Gartenzaun
mich einsperren, mich aussperrn will.

The Scarecrows

I don't know whether earth can be bought,
whether it's enough to bury four posts,
with a little rust between them and some shrubs,
in the sand, and call the thing a garden.

I don't know what the starlings think.
Sometimes they flutter up, disperse,
sprinkle my afternoon,
pretend that one can scare them off,
as though scarecrows were scarecrows
and air guns behind the curtains
and cats in the beanrows.

I don't know what the old jackets
and those trouser pockets know about us.
I don't know what broods inside hats,
for what thoughts something is hatched
and fledges and won't let itself be scared off;
by scarecrows in any case we are guarded.

Are scarecrows mammals?
It does look as though they multiplied
by swapping hats overnight:
already three of them stand in my garden,
bow, and politely wave to me
and turn about and wink at the sun
and talk, talk to the lettuces.

I don't know whether my garden fence
wants to shut me in or out.

Ich weiß nicht, was das Unkraut will,
weiß nicht, was jene Blattlaus will bedeuten,
weiß nicht, ob alte Jacken, alte Hosen,
wenn sie mit Löffeln in den Dosen
rostig und blechern windwärts läuten,
zur Vesper, ob zum Ave läuten,
zum Aufstand aller Vogelscheuchen läuten.

I don't know what the weeds want,
don't know what that greenfly signifies,
don't know whether old jackets, old trousers
when with their spoons rusty and tinny
windward they ring, to vespers or ave they ring
or to the insurrection of every scarecrow.

Kleine Aufforderung zum grossen
Mundaufmachen – oder der Wasserspeier spricht

Wer jene Fäulnis,
die lange hinter der Zahnpaste lebte,
freigeben, ausatmen will,
muß seinen Mund aufmachen.

Wir wollen nun den Mund aufmachen,
die schlimmen Goldzähne,
die wir den Toten brachen und pflückten,
auf Ämtern abliefern.

Um dicke Väter
– jetzt, da auch wir schon Väter und immer dicker –
absetzen und ausspeien zu können,
muß man den Mund aufmachen;

wie unsere Kinder bei Zeiten
den Mund aufmachen, die große Fäulnis,
die schlimmen Goldzähne, die dicken Väter
ausspeien werden, absetzen werden.

Little Address Calling for a Great Opening
of Mouths – or the Gargoyle Speaks

Whoever wishes
to release, to breathe out
that caries which long has lurked behind the toothpaste
has no choice but to open his mouth.

Now let us open our mouths,
go to offices and hand in
the bad gold teeth
which we broke and plucked from the dead.

Before you can hope to
depose, to spew out fat fathers –
now that we too are fathers and putting on fat –
you've no choice but to open your mouths;

just as our children in time will
open their mouths, will depose,
will spew out the great caries,
the bad gold teeth, the fat fathers.

Köche und Löffel

Und manche sagen: Koch ist Koch.
Neu, frischgewaschen und gestärkt,
im Schneefall und vor heller Wand
bleiben die Köche unbemerkt,
und nur der Löffel in der Hand
rührt uns, läßt niemanden vergessen:
Die Köche geben uns zu essen.

Wir sollten nicht von Suppen sprechen
– der Suppenkohl kann nicht dafür –
denn Hunger heißt nur, Vorwand für ein Bier,
und Überdruß leckt jedem Löffel Flächen
und sitzt und zählt die Schritte bis zur Tür.

Die Puppen überleben sich,
der Hahn stirbt vor dem Koch
und kräht woanders, dennoch zittern
in dieser Stadt manchmal die Scheiben.
Die Puppen überleben sich,
der Hahn stirbt vor dem Koch.

Es liegt am Fleisch, der Koch lebt nur im Geist.
Die Zeit vergeht, das Rindfleisch wird nicht weich,
wird später, wird im Schlaf noch dauern,
wird zwischen deinen Zähnen kauern;
es liegt am Fleisch, der Koch lebt nur im Geist.

Sie legten beide, jeder legte sich,
sie legten sich zusammen in den Löffel,
nur weil er hohl war, Schlaf vortäuschte,

Chefs and Spoons

And some will say: a chef's a chef.
All newly laundered, starched and spry
in snowfall or against a wall
that's whitewashed, chefs escape the eye
and then the spoons they hold are all
that stirs us, leaves us in no doubt:
the things we eat, the chefs dish out.

I don't think we should talk of soup
– the cabbage stock is neither here nor there –
for hunger is mere pretext for a beer,
and glut licks large and small spoons out of shape
and sits and counts the paces to the door.

The dolls outlive themselves,
the cockerel dies before the chef
and crows elsewhere, and yet at times
the window panes will shiver in this town.
The dolls outlive themselves,
the cockerel dies before the chef.

Flesh is the cause, a chef lives but in spirit.
Time passes, but the beef is still not done,
will last till later, till you sleep,
between your teeth will creep and lurk;
flesh is the cause, a chef lives but in spirit.

They both lay down, each one of them lay down,
together in the spoon they both lay down,
for it was hollow and it promised sleep –

– auch hohl war Vorwand und nur Widerspruch –
der Schlaf blieb kurz und kurz vorm Überkochen
hat beide, und ein jeder lag alleine,
derselbe Löffel abgeschöpft.

Hier ist kein Tod, der nicht zum Löffel führt,
und keine Liebe, die nicht ausgehöhlt
an Löffeln leidet und im Löffel bebt,
sich dreht, worum dreht, da sich alles
mit Löffeln nur um Löffel dreht.

Bleib Löffel, geh.
Wem Löffel, Löffel führt wohin.
Wann Löffel, Löffel kam zu spät.
Wer rührt mich, rührt mich und wohin.
Über und über wen balbiert.
Bleib, Löffel, geh – und sag mir nicht wohin.

So lernst du langsam Löffel unterscheiden,
kannst dich in Schubladen nicht mehr vermeiden,
du löffelst mit und läßt dich gern vertauschen,
du gibst dich blechern, gleichst dich an,
hörst deinen Nachbarn, wolltest gar nicht lauschen,
doch Löffel liegt dem Löffel an.

yet hollow too was pretext and mere contradiction –
their sleep was short and shortly before boiling over
both, and now each one lay alone,
the self-same spoon skimmed off.

No death is here but leads back to the spoon,
and no love here but, hollowed out, at last
suffers from spoons and trembles in the spoon,
revolves, revolves round what, since everything
with spoons revolves round spoons and only spoons.

Then stay, spoon, go.
To whom spoon, spoon leads where.
What time spoon, spoon was late.
Who stirs me, stirs me where.
Over and over cuts whose hair.
Then stay, spoon, go – and do not tell me where.

So gradually you learn to tell the spoons apart,
no longer can avoid yourself in drawers,
spoon with the rest and like to be mistaken,
act tinny and assimilate yourself,
can hear your neighbour, never meant to eavesdrop,
yet spoon fits into spoon, lies close to spoon.

Zauberei mit den Bräuten Christi

Aus himmlischen Töpfen

Wer hat dieses Spielchen ausgedacht?
Die Köche springen in den Hof,
erschrecken die Nonnen
oder auf Treppen fassen sie zu,
im Keller, im Speicher,
auf Gängen atemlos,
Hände behaart,
mit Löffeln schlagen sie
und rühren auf,
was gerade sich setzte,
und schöpfen ab, was ihm galt –
dem Bräutigam.

Theater

Köche, Nonnen und Vögel,
dann Wind aus der Kulisse,
und ganz am Anfang bricht ein Glas,
daß Scherben noch genug sind, wenn am Ende
die Nonnen flüchten – Kurs Südost. –
Auch Vögel kommen meistens in den Himmel,
weil sie den Köchen und dem Wind
an Federn überlegen sind.

Magical Exercise with the Brides of Christ

Out of Celestial Pots

Who thought up this little game?
The chefs leap into the courtyard,
startle the nuns
or grab at them on the staircase,
in the cellar, in the attic,
in passages, breathless,
with hairy hands
with spoons they beat
and stir up
what was about to settle,
and skim off what concerned him –
the Bridegroom.

Theatre

Chefs, nuns and birds,
then a wind from the wings
and right at the beginning a glass breaks
so that there are shards enough when at the end
the nuns take flight – their course southeasterly.
Birds too usually go to Heaven,
because in plumage they are superior
to chefs and the wind

Vorsicht

Ergingen Nonnen sich am Strand
und hielten mit gewaschnen Händen
schwarz Regenschirme,
daß die Hitze
nicht Einfalt bräune. –
Kleine Füße traten Muscheln,
daß kein Ohr sei,
wenn Agneta, die Novize, sich verspräche,
was oft vorkommt.

Keine Taube

Es begegneten sich eine Möwe
und eine Nonne.
Und die Möwe
hackte der Nonne die Augen aus.
Die Nonne aber hob ihren Schleier,
lud wie Maria den Wind ein,
segelte blind und davon. –
Blieb der katholische Strand,
glaubte an blendende Segel,
Muschel rief Muschel ins Ohr:
Geliebte im Herrn und am Strand,
erschien ihr der heilige Geist
auch nicht in Gestalt einer Taube,
so schlug er doch weiß, daß ich glaube.

Caution

Nuns disported themselves on the beach
and in washed hands held
black umbrellas,
so that the heat
would not tan innocence.
Little feet trod on shells,
so that there would be no ear
when Agneta, the novice, stumbled over words
as she often does.

No Dove

A seagull and a nun
met.
And the seagull
hacked out the nun's eyes.
But the nun lifted her veil,
like Mary invited the wind,
blindly sailed up and away –
What remained was the Catholic beach,
it believed in dazzling sails,
seashell cried into seashell's ear:
Beloved in the Lord and on the beach,
if not in the guise of a dove
yet the Holy Spirit appeared to her,
and white those wings beat, so that I may believe.

Die Nonnen

Sie sind nur für den Wind gemacht.
Sie segeln immer, ohne auch zu loten.
Was ihnen himmlisch Bräutigam,
heißt andernorts Klabautermann.
Ich sah einst Nonnen,
eine ganze Flotte.
Sie wehten fort zum Horizont.
Ein schöner Tag, ein Segeltag,
tags drauf Trafalgar, die Armada sank.
Was wußte Nelson schon von Nonnen.

The Nuns

They are made for the wind.
They always sail, even without sounding the depth.
What to them is the Celestial Bridegroom
elsewhere is known as the Ship's Hobgoblin.
I once saw nuns,
a whole fleet of them.
They wafted off to the horizon.
A fine day, a day for sailing,
the day after, Trafalgar, the Armada sank.
What, after all, did Nelson know about nuns.

Die Seeschlacht

Ein amerikanischer Flugzeugträger
und eine gotische Kathedrale
versenkten sich
mitten im Stillen Ozean
gegenseitig.
Bis zum Schluß
spielte der junge Vikar auf der Orgel. –
Nun hängen Flugzeuge und Engel in der Luft
und können nicht landen.

The Sea Battle

An American aircraft carrier
and a Gothic cathedral
simultaneously sank each other
in the middle of the Pacific.
To the last
the young curate played on the organ.
Now aeroplanes and angels hang in the air
and have nowhere to land.

Aus dem Alltag der Puppe Nana

Die Uhr

Die Puppe spielt mit den Minuten,
doch niemand spielt mehr mit der Puppe, –
es sei denn, daß die Uhr drei Schritte macht
und Nana sagt: Nana Nana Nana ...

Die Frisur

Die Puppe spielt mit dem Regen,
sie flicht ihn, sie hängt ihn sich, Zöpfe, ums Ohr
und holt aus dem Kästchen den Kamm hervor
und kämmt mit dem Kamm den Regen.

Bei Vollmond

Die Puppe wacht, die Kinder schlafen,
der Mond, verwickelt in Gardinen,
die Puppe hilft und rückt an den Gardinen,
der Mond verdrückt sich und die Puppe wacht.

Schwüler Tag

Die Puppe bekam einen Zollstock geschenkt,
der war gelb, und so spielt sie Gewitter.
Sie knickte den Meter, dem Blitz glich er sehr, –
nur donnern, das fiel der Puppe sehr schwer.

From the Daily Life of the Doll Nana

The Clock

The doll is playing with the minutes,
but no one now plays with the doll –
except at times when the clock takes three steps
and Nana whimpers: Nana, Nana, Nana . . .

Her Hair Style

The doll is playing with the rain,
she plaits it, hangs it as pigtails round her ears
and from the little box takes the comb
and with the comb she combs the rain.

In the Light of the Full Moon

The doll's awake, the children sleep,
the moon, entangled in the curtains,
the doll helps out and pulls at the curtains,
the moon slinks off and the doll wakes.

Sultry Day

Somebody gave the doll a ruler,
it was yellow, so she plays at thunderstorms.
She bent the yardstick, it was much like lightning –
only thundering was very hard for the doll.

Die Tollwut

Die Puppe fand einen ledigen Zahn,
den legte sie in ein Glas.
Da sprang das Glas, der Zahn wieder frei
biß einem Stuhl die Waden entzwei.

Schicksal

Die Puppe spielt mit der Spinne,
die Spinne spielt Jojo.
Die Puppe grieft nach dem Faden,
das könnte uns allen schaden,
so viel hängt an dem Faden.

Frühling

Die Puppe freut sich, Zelluloid,
es tropft vom Dach auf ihren Kopf
und macht ein Loch, –
die Puppe freut sich, Zelluloid.

Herbst

Die Puppe spielt mit den Prozenten,
der Kurs, die Pappel zittert.
Die Blätter, bunte Scheine fallen ab,
die deutsche Mark verwittert.

Im Zoo

Die Puppe ging in den Zoo
und sah der Eule ins Auge.

Rabies

The doll found an unattached tooth,
she put it inside a glass.
The glass cracked, the tooth, released from there,
bit right through the calves of a chair.

Destiny

The doll is playing with the spider,
the spider is playing yo-yo.
The doll grabs at the string, for us all
that could be a very bad thing,
so much depends on the string.

Spring

The doll is happy, celluloid,
a drip from the roof falls on her head
and makes a hole –
the doll is happy, celluloid.

Autumn

The doll is playing with per cents,
the rate, the aspen sways.
The leafage, multicoloured stones, drops off,
the German mark decays.

At the Zoo

The doll went to the zoo
and looked the owl in the eye.

Seitdem hat die Puppe Mäuse im Blick
und wünscht sich in Voreulenzeiten zurück.

Das lange Lied

Die Puppe singt die Tapete.
Doch weil die Tapete so viele Strophen hat,
wird die Puppe bald heiser sein. –
Wer wird die Tapete zu Ende singen?

Vorsichtige Liebe

Die Puppe saß unter dem Bett der Eltern und hörte alles.
Als sie es mit dem Schaukelpferd gleichtun wollte,
sagte sie zwischendurch immer wieder:
Paß aber auf, hörst du, paß aber auf.

Schlechte Schützen

Die Puppe wurde auf ein Brett genagelt
und mit Pfeilen beworfen.
Doch kein Pfeil traf,
weil die Puppe schielte.

Der Torso

Die Puppe hatte keine Arme mehr,
und als auch die Beine auswanderten,
überlegte sie lange, ob sie im Lande bleiben sollte. –
Sie blieb und sagte: Es geht doch nichts über Europa.

Since then the owl has had mice in view
and has wished she were back in the pre-owl age.

The Long Song

The doll is singing the wallpaper.
But since the wallpaper has so many stanzas
the doll will soon be hoarse.
Who will sing the wallpaper to the end?

Cautious Love

The doll sat under the parents' bed and heard everything.
When she wanted to do the same with the rocking-horse
she kept saying in between again and again:
Be careful, though, do you hear, be careful.

Poor Shots

The doll was nailed on to a board
and arrows aimed at her.
But no arrow hit her,
because the doll had a squint.

The Torso

The doll had no arms left,
and when the legs emigrated also
she wondered for a long time whether she should stay in her
    country.
She stayed and said: There's no place like Europe.

Wachstum

Die Puppe wächst und übersieht die Schränke.
Die Bälle springen, doch die Puppe lacht
von oben und die Kinder staunen unten
und hätten das von ihrer Puppe nie gedacht.

Die letzte Predigt

Die Puppe spricht, die müden Automaten
verstummen und rappeln nicht mehr Pfefferminz;
die Häuser fallen schwer aufs Knie
und werden fromm – nur weil die Puppe spricht.

Nachmittag

Die Puppe fiel in den Tee,
zerging wie der Zucker im Tee –
und die ihn tranken entpuppten sich,
bis einer des anderen Puppe glich.

In Memoriam

Die Puppe kostete zwei Mark und zehn, –
für diesen Preis schien sie uns schön.
Selbst solltet ihr schönere Puppen sehn,
so kosten sie mehr als zwei Mark und zehn.

Growth

The doll is growing and looks down at the wardrobes.
The balls are jumping, but the doll laughs
from up above and the children wonder at it from down below
and never would have thought it of their doll.

The Last Sermon

The doll is speaking, the weary slot machines
fall silent and no longer rattle with peppermint;
the houses heavily drop on their knees
and grow devout – only because the doll is speaking.

Afternoon

The doll fell into the tea,
dissolved like sugar in tea –
and those who drank it so changed their shapes
that one of them looked like the other's doll.

In Memoriam

The doll cost 2.20 marks when new –
for that price to us it seemed beautiful too.
If you could find a doll still more pretty,
you'd have to pay more for it now in this city.

Mein Radiergummi

Mit den Augen meines Radiergummis gesehen
ist Berlin eine schöne Stadt.

An einem Sonntag,
ganz erfüllt von Zahnschmerz und Überdruß,
sagte ich zu meinem Radiergummi:
Wir sollten verreisen, uns,
wie du es nennst, verkrümeln
und unseren Zahnschmerz verteilen.

Immer dem Aschenbecher gegenüber
haben wir uns aufgerieben:
Meine Taschen sind voller Eintrittskarten –
ich kann den Schlüssel nicht mehr finden.

Verlust

Gestern verlor ich meinen Radiergummi;
ohne ihn bin ich hilflos.
Meine Frau frägt: Was ist?
Ich antworte: Was soll sein?
Ich habe meinen Radiergummi verloren.

Gefunden

Man fand meinen Radiergummi.
In der Ruine des Lehrter Bahnhofes
half er den Abbrucharbeitern:
Klein ist er geworden
und nicht mehr zu gebrauchen.

My Eraser

Seen with the eyes of my eraser
Berlin is a beautiful city.

One Sunday,
entirely taken up with toothache and low spirits,
I said to my eraser:
We ought to take a journey, make,
as you say, ourselves scarce,
and dissipate our toothache.

Always facing the ashtray
we have worn ourselves out:
my pockets are full of entrance tickets –
I can't find the key any more.

Loss

Yesterday I lost my eraser;
without it I'm helpless.
My wife asks: What's up?
I answer: What should be up?
I've lost my eraser.

Found

My eraser was found.
In the ruins of Lehrter Station
it was helping the demolition workers:
it's grown small
and no good for anything.

Teamwork

Heute kaufte ich einen neuen Radiergummi,
legte ihn auf ein verbrauchtes Papier
und sah ihm zu.
Ich und mein Radiergummi, wir sind sehr fleißig,
arbeiten Hand in Hand.

Am Nachmittag

Wenn mein Radiergummi schläft,
schaffe ich mit beiden Händen.
Die Zeit will genutzt sein:
Mein Radiergummi schläft nur selten.

Ungläubig

Manche sagen, man könne die falschen Striche stehen lassen;
doch mein Radiergummi
läuft selbst den richtigen hinterdrein.
Kürzlich wollt er das Übel zuhause treffen
und hat meinem Bleistift das Mark ausgesogen,
daß er jetzt daliegt: hohl und nicht mehr anzuspitzen.

Nachts

Bald ist es nicht mehr so hell
über den Dächern und Kaminen.
Mein Radiergummi und der Mond,
beide nehmen ab.

Teamwork

Today I bought a new eraser,
laid it on a sheet of used paper
and watched it.
I and my eraser are very busy,
working hand in hand.

In the Afternoon

When my eraser sleeps
I work with both hands.
One mustn't waste time:
My eraser sleeps only rarely.

Incredulous

Some people say one can leave the wrong strokes unchanged,
but my eraser
runs after even the right ones.
Lately it wanted to catch the troublemaker at home
and sucked the marrow out of my pencil,
so that it lies there now: hollow and not to be sharpened.

At Night

Soon it won't be so bright
above the roofs and fireplaces.
My eraser and the moon,
both are on the wane.

[55]

Abschied

Heute kaufte ich mir für Geld einen neuen Radiergummi.
Noch trage ich ihn in der Tasche, trage ihn hin und her.
Noch fühlen meine Spuren sich sicher, laufen mir nach –
wie einst ein Kellner mir nachlief, dem ich zu zahlen vergaß.

Heute kaufte ich mir für Geld
einen neuen Radiergummi.
Spurlos verkrümelte ich,
mein Bier bezahlte der Kellner.

Farewell

Today for money I bought myself a new eraser.
Still I carry it in my pocket, carry it to and fro.
Still my tracks feel secure, run after me –
as a waiter did once, when I forgot to pay.

Today for money I bought
myself a new eraser.
Without trace I made myself scarce,
the waiter paid for my beer.

Die Grosse Trümmerfrau Spricht

Gnade Gnade.
Die große Trümmerfrau
hat einen Plan entworfen,
dem jeder Stein unterliegen wird.
Der große Ziegelbrenner will mitmachen.

Die Stadt die Stadt.
Hingestreut liegt Berlin,
lehnt sich mit Brandmauern gegen Winde,
die aus Ost Süd West, aus dem Norden kommen
und die Stadt befreien wollen.

Hier drüben hier
und drüben hängen die Herzen
an einem einzigen Bindfaden,
hüpfen und werden gehüpft, wenn Trümmerfrau
und Ziegelbrenner ihre Liebe zu Faden schlagen.

Liebe Liebe
spielten einst Trümmerfrauen,
rieben mit Schenkeln
Klinker und Ziegel
zu Splitt Mehl Staub Liebe.

Wo wo wo wo
sind die alten Galane geblieben,
wo wilhelminischer Mörtel?
Jahrgänge Jahrgänge –
doch Trümmerfrauen sind keine Weinkenner.

The Great Rubblewoman Speaks

Mercy mercy.
The great rubblewoman
has conceived a plan
to which every stone will have to submit.
The great brickburner wants to join in.

Our city our city.
All scattered lies Berlin,
leans with its fire walls against winds
that come from east south west, and from the north,
wishing to liberate the city.

Here over there here
and over there hearts hang
by a single length of string,
hop and are hopped, when rubblewoman
and brickburner beat their love into threads.

Love love
at one time rubblewomen played at,
with their thighs rubbed
clinker and brick
into chippings flour dust love.

Where where where where
have the old gallants gone,
where Kaiser Wilhelm's mortar?
Vintage years vintage years –
but rubblewomen are no connoisseurs of wine.

Flaute Flaute
schreien die Trümmerfrauen
und lassen den letzten
wundertätigen Ziegelstein
zwischen den Zähnen knirschen.

Splitt Splitt Splitt Splitt.
Nur noch wenn Zwiebeln
oder ein kleineres Leid
uns mit Tränen versorgen,
tritt Ziegelsplitt aufs Augenlid.

Sonderbar sonderbar
sehen dann Neubauten aus,
zittern ein wenig, erwarten
den klassisch zu nennenden Schlag
mit der Handkante in die Kniekehle.

Sie sie sie sie
gräbt den Sand unterm Pfeiler weg.
Sie sag ich sie
spuckt in die trächtigen
Betonmischmaschinen.

Sie sie sie sie
hat das große Gelächter erfunden.
Wenn immer die große Trümmerfrau lacht,
klemmen Fahrstühle, springen Heizkörper,
weinen die kleinen verwöhnten Baumeister.

Mir gab sie mir,
ihrem ängstlich beflissenen Ziegelersatz,
gab sie den Auftrag,

Stagnation stagnation
shriek the rubblewomen
and make the last
miraculous brick
grate between their teeth.

Chippings chippings chippings chippings
Only now when onions
or a smaller sorrow
supply us with tears
do fresh chippings touch our eyelids.

Strange strange
then the new buildings look,
tremble a little, await
the blow you'd call classical
with the side of the hand into the knee's hollow.

She she she she
digs away the sand under the pillar.
She I say she
spits into the pregnant
concrete mixers.

She she she she
has invented the great laughter.
Whenever the great rubblewoman laughs
elevators jam, radiators burst,
the small pampered architects weep.

To me, to me she gave,
her timidly hardworking brick substitute,
she gave the commission

[61]

Wind zu machen, Staub zu machen
und ernsthaft für ihr Gelächter zu werben.

Ich ich ich ich
stand abseits,
hatte die Brandmauer im Auge,
und die Brandmauer
hatte mich im Auge.

Ging ging ging ging
von weit her
auf die Brandmauer los,
als wollte ich
die Brandmauer durchschreiten.

Nahm nahm nahm nahm
einen Anlauf,
der viel versprach;
jene Brandmauer aber war neunzehn Meter breit
und zweiundzwanzig Meter hoch.

Schlug schlug schlug schlug
an der Mauer
mein Wasser ab,
daß es rauschte
und hörte dem zu.

Werbung Werbung
rauschte die Brandmauer.
Niemand will mich als Werbefläche
mieten, haushoch beschriften
und werben lassen.

to make wind, to make dust
and seriously promote her laughter.

I I I I
stood aside,
kept my eye on the fire wall,
and the fire wall
kept its eye on me.

Went went went went
from far off
went for the fire wall,
as though I wanted
to walk through the fire wall.

Took took took took
a long run
that was most promising,
but that fire wall was nineteen metres wide
and twenty-two metres high.

Made made made made
water against
that wall,
so that it roared,
and listened to that.

Sales promotion sales promotion
the fire wall roared,
no one wants to hire me as
a billboard, letter me house-high
and let me promote sales.

Ich ich ich ich
will allen Brandmauern,
die nordwärts schauen,
riesengroß Trümmerfrauen
malen oder auch einbrennen.

Trümmerfrau Trümmerfrau
– sollen die Kinder singen –
hat mit dem Ziegelbrenner Ziegelbrenner
einen ganz neuen Plan gemacht.
Alle Steine wissen Bescheid.

Ziegelbrenner Ziegelbrenner
– sollen die Kinder singen –
geht nachts mit der Trümmerfrau Trümmerfrau
durch die Stadt
und schätzt die Stadt ab.

Trümmerfrau Trümmerfrau
– singen die Kinder –
will mit dem Ziegelbrenner Ziegelbrenner
heut eine Wette machen Wette machen –
es geht um viel Schutt.

Lamento Lamento –
die große Trümmerfrau singt ihr Lamento.
Doch alle Sender, drüben und hier,
-senden von früh bis spät nur jenen alten
beschissenen Walzerkönig.

I I I I
want to paint onto or burn
into all fire walls that face north
gigantic
rubblewomen.

Rubblewoman rubblewoman
– the children are to sing –
together with the brickburner brickburner
has hatched a wholly new plan
All the stones know all about it.

Brickburner brickburner
– the children are to sing –
at night walks with the rubblewoman rubblewoman
through the city
and assesses its value.

Rubblewoman rubblewoman
– the children sing –
with the brickburner brickburner
wants to lay a bet lay a bet today –
much rubble is at stake.

Lamentation lamentation –
the great rubblewoman sings her lamentation.
But all the radio stations, over there and here,
from morning to night only transmit
that shitty old king of waltzes.

Tot sie ist tot
sagen die Baumeister,
verschweigen aber, daß eine unabwendbare Hand
Mittag für Mittag löffelweis toten Mörtel
in ihre Suppen mengt.

Amen Amen.
Hingestreut liegt Berlin.
Staub fliegt auf,
dann wieder Flaute.
Die große Trümmerfrau wird heiliggesprochen.

Dead she is dead
the architects say,
but do not say that an ineluctable hand
noon after noon mixes by spoonfuls
dead mortar into their soups.

Amen Amen.
All scattered lies Berlin.
Dust flies up,
then stagnation again.
The great rubblewoman is canonized.

Ehe

Wir haben Kinder, das zählt bis zwei.
Meistens gehen wir in verschiedene Filme.
Vom Auseinanderleben sprechen die Freunde.
  Doch meine und Deine Interessen
  berühren sich immer noch
  an immer den gleichen Stellen.
  Nicht nur die Frage nach den Manschettenknöpfen.
  Auch Dienstleistungen:
  Halt mal den Spiegel.
  Glühbirnen auswechseln.
  Etwas abholen.
  Oder Gespräche, bis alles besprochen ist.
Zwei Sender, die manchmal gleichzeitig
auf Empfang gestellt sind.
Soll ich abschalten?
  Erschöpfung lügt Harmonie.
  Was sind wir uns schuldig? Das.
  Ich mag das nicht: Deine Haare im Klo.
Aber nach elf Jahren noch Spass an der Sache.
Ein Fleisch sein bei schwankenden Preisen.
Wir denken sparsam in Kleingeld.
Im Dunkeln glaubst Du mir alles.
Aufribbeln und Neustricken.
Gedehnte Vorsicht.
Dankeschönsagen.
  Nimm Dich zusammen.
  Dein Rasen vor unserem Haus.
  Jetzt bist Du wieder ironisch.
  Lach doch darüber.
  Hau doch ab, wenn Du kannst.
  Unser Hass ist witterungsbeständig.

Marriage

We have children, that counts up to two.
We usually go to different films.
It's friends who talk of our drifting apart.
   But your interests and mine
   still touch, at the same points always.
   Not only the question about cufflinks.
   Little services too:
   Just hold that mirror.
   Change the bulbs.
   Fetch something.
   Or discussions, till everything is discussed.
Two stations that at times
are both tuned in to receive.
Shall I turn myself off?
   Exhaustion simulates harmony.
   What do we owe each other? That.
   I don't like that – your hairs in the john.
But after eleven years the thing is still fun.
To be one flesh when prices fluctuate.
We think thriftily, in small coin.
In the dark you believe all I say.
Unpicking and knitting anew.
A stretched cautiousness.
Saying thank you.
   Pull yourself together.
   That lawn of yours in our garden.
   Now you're being ironic again.
   Why don't you laugh about it?
   Clear out, then, if you can.
   Our hatred is weatherproof.

Doch manchmal, zerstreut, sind wir zärtlich.
Die Zeugnisse der Kinder
müssen unterschrieben werden.
Wir setzen uns von der Steuer ab.
Erst übermorgen ist Schluss.
Du. Ja Du. Rauch nicht so viel.

But sometimes, distrait, we are tender.
The children's reports
have to be signed.
    We deduct each other from income tax.
    Not till the day after tomorrow will it be over.
    You. Yes, you. Don't smoke so much.

Plötzliche Angst

Wenn sich im Sommer bei östlichem Wind
   Septemberstaub rührt und in verspäteter Zeitung
   die Kommentare Mystisches streifen,

wenn sich die Mächte umbetten wollen
   und zur Kontrolle neue Geräte
   öffentlich zeugen dürfen,

wenn um den Fussball Urlauber zelten
   und der Nationen verspielter Blick
   grosse Entscheidungen spiegelt,

wenn Zahlenkolonnen den Schlaf erzwingen
   und durch die Träume getarnter Feind
   atmet, auf Ellbogen robbt,

wenn in Gesprächen immer das gleiche Wort
   aufgespart in der Hinterhand bleibt
   und ein Zündhölzlein Mittel zum Schreck wird,

wenn sich beim Schwimmen in Rückenlage
   himmelwärts nur der Himmel türmt,
   suchen die Ängstlichen rasch das Ufer,

liegt plötzliche Angst in der Luft.

Sudden Fright

When in summer in an easterly wind
   September dust whirls and in the belated paper
      editorials are almost mystical,

when the powers want to change beds
   and are allowed to beget openly
      new instruments for control,

when around footballs holiday-makers camp
   and the playful glance of the nations
      mirrors weighty decisions,

when columns of figures put one to sleep
   and through dreams a camouflaged enemy
      breathes, and crawls nearer,

when in conversations always the same word
   is backhandedly held in reserve
      and a match can strike terror,

when from the backstroke position in swimming
   skyward only the sky seems to tower,
      frightened people hurry back to the shore,

a sudden fright hangs in the air.

König Lear

In der Halle,
in jeder Hotelhalle,
in einem eingesessenen Sessel,
Klub-, Leder-, doch niemals Korbsessel,
zwischen verfrühten Kongressteilnehmern
und leeren Sesseln, die Anteil haben,
selten, dann mit Distanz gegrüsst,
sitzt er, die von Kellnern umsegelte Insel,
und vergisst nichts.

Diese Trauer findet an sich Geschmack
und lacht mit zwölf Muskeln einerseits.
Viel hört er nicht aber alles
und widerlegt den Teppich.
Die Stukkatur denkt er weg
und stemmt seine Brauen gegen.
Bis sich ihr Blattgold löst,
sprechen Barockengel vor.
Die Kirche schickt Spitzel;
ihm fehlen Komparsen.
Vergeblich ahmen zuviele Spiegel ihn nach.
Seine Töchter sind Anekdoten.

Im Hotel Sacher wird nach Herrn Kortner verlangt.
Herr Kortner lässt sagen, er sei auf der Probe.
In der Halle, in seinem Sessel, stellt jemand sich tot
und trifft sich mit Kent auf der Heide.

King Lear

In the hall
in any hotel hall
in a chair that sags with long use,
club, leather, but never basket chair,
amid premature participants in congresses
and empty armchairs that play their part,
rarely addressed and, if so, with reserve,
he sits,
an island skirted by cruising waiters,
and forgets nothing.

This grief takes pleasure in itself
and laughs with twelve muscles on the one side.
He does not hear much but everything
and refutes the carpet.
His mind rips off the stucco work
and his eyebrows push it away.
Till their gold leaf peels off
baroque angels present themselves.
The church sends informers;
what he lacks is walk-ons.
In vain too many mirrors copy him.
His daughters are anecdotes.

In Hotel Sacher Herr Kortner is paged.
Herr Kortner is busy rehearsing, he has them say.
In the hall, in his armchair, someone acts dead
and goes to meet Kent on the heath.

Schlaflos

Mein Atem verfehlte das Nadelöhr.
Jetzt muss ich zählen
und heimwärts blättern treppab.

Aber die Kriechgänge
münden in Wassergräben,
in denen Kaulquappen ...
Zähl doch mal nach.

Meine Rückspule plappert ihr drittes Jahrzehnt.
Das Bett geht auf Reisen. Und überall legt
der Zoll seine Hand auf: Was führen sie mit?

Drei Strümpfe, fünf Schuhe, ein Nebelgerät. –
Mehrsprachig werden sie nachgezählt:
die Sterne, die Schafe, die Panzer, die Stimmen ...
Ein Zwischenergebnis wird ausgezählt.

Sleepless

My breath missed the needle's eye.
Now I must count
and homeward leaf down the stairs.

But the crawling forays
end in watery ditches,
in which tadpoles . . .
Count up again.

My playback reel gabbles its third decade.
The bed leaves for a journey. And everywhere
The Customs interpose: What's in your luggage?

Three socks, five shoes, a fog machine –
In several languages they are counted up:
the stars, the sheep, the tanks, the voices . . .
A provisional sum is counted out.

Liebe

Das ist es:
Der bargeldlose Verkehr.
Die immer zu kurze Decke.
Der Wackelkontakt.

Hinter dem Horizont suchen.
Im Laub mit vier Schuhen rascheln
und in Gedanken Barfüsse reiben.
Herzen vermieten und mieten;
oder im Zimmer mit Dusche und Spiegel,
im Leihwagen, Kühler zum Mond,
wo immer die Unschuld absteigt
und ihr Programm verbrennt,
fistelt das Wort
jedesmal anders und neu.

Heute, vor noch geschlossener Kasse,
knisterten Hand in Hand
der gedrückte Greis und die zierliche Greisin.
Der Film versprach Liebe.

Love

That's it:
The cashless commerce.
The blanket always too short.
The loose connection.

To search behind the horizon.
To brush fallen leaves with four shoes
and in one's mind to rub bare feet.
To let and to rent hearts;
or in a room with shower and mirror,
in a hired car, bonnet facing the moon,
wherever innocence stops
and burns its programme,
the word in falsetto sounds
different and new each time.

Today, in front of a box office not yet open,
hand in hand crackled
the hangdog old man and the dainty old woman.
The film promised love.

Hymme

So kompliziert wie eine Nachtigall,
so blechern wie,
gutmütig wie,
so knitterfrei, althergebracht,
so grün ernst sauer, so durchwachsen,
so ebenmässig,
so behaart,
so nah dem Wasser, windgerecht,
so feuerfest, oft umgegraben,
so kinderleicht, zerlesen wie,
so neu und knarrend, teuer wie,
so unterkellert, häuslich wie,
so leicht verloren, blankgegriffen,
so dünn geblasen, schneegekühlt,
so eigenhändig, mündig wie,
so herzlos wie,
so sterblich wie,
so einfach wie meine Seele.

Hymn

As complicated as a nightingale,
as tinny as,
kind-hearted as,
as crease-proof, as traditional,
as green grave sour, as streaky,
as symmetrical,
as hairy,
as near the water, true to the wind,
as fireproof, frequently turned over,
as childishly easy, well-thumbed as,
as new and creaking, expensive as,
as deeply cellared, domestic as,
as easily lost, shiny with use,
as thinly blown, as snow-chilled as,
as independent, as mature,
as heartless as,
as mortal as,
as simple as my soul.

Schreiben

In Wirklichkeit
  war das Glas nur hüfthoch gefüllt.
    Vollschlank geneigt. Im Bodensatz liegt.
Silben stechen.
Neben dem Müllschlucker wohnen
und zwischen Gestank und Geruch ermitteln.
Dem Kuchen die Springform nehmen.
Bücher,
  in ihren Gestellen,
    können nicht umfallen.
Das, oft unterbrochen, sind meine Gedanken.
Wann wird die Milch komisch?
Im Krebsgang den Fortschritt messen.
Abwarten, bis das Metall ermüdet.
Die Brücke langsam.
  zum Mitschreiben,
    einstürzen lassen.
Vorher den Schrottwert errechnen.
Sätze verabschieden Sätze.
Wenn Politik
  dem Wetter
    zur Aussage wird:
Ein Hoch über Rußland.
Zuhause
  verreist sein; auf Reisen
  zuhause bleiben.
Wir wechseln das Klima nicht.
Nur Einfalt
  will etwas beleben,
    für tot erklären.

Writing

In reality
    the glass was filled only hip-high.
        Plump, well-rounded. Lies in the dregs.
Engrave syllables.
Live next to the garbage disposal unit
and distinguish between a stench and a smell.
Deprive the cake of its springform.
Books
    in their cases
        can't fall over.
That, often interrupted, is how my thoughts went.
When does the milk grow funny?
Measure progress in crayfish gait.
Wait patiently until metal tires.
Let the bridge slowly,
    so that the writing keeps pace,
        collapse.
Before that, calculate its value as scrap.
Sentences bid farewell to sentences.
When politics
    become
        the weather's way of speaking:
A high-pressure belt over Russia.
At home
    to have gone abroad; on travels
    to remain at home.
We will not change the climate.
Only naïveté
    wants to make something live,
        declare it dead.

Dumm sein, immer neu anfangen wollen.
Erinnere mich bitte, sobald ich Heuschnupfen
oder der Blumenkorso in Zoppot sage.
Rückblickend aus dem Fenster schauen.
Reime auf Schnepfendreck.
Jeden Unsinn laut mitsprechen.
Urbin, ich hab's! – Urbin, ich hab's!
Das Ungenaue genau treffen.
Die Taschen
   sind voller alter Eintrittskarten.
      Wo ist der Zündschlüssel?
Den Zündschlüssel streichen.
Mitleid mit Verben.
An den Radiergummi glauben.
Im Fundbüro einen Schirm beschwören.
Mit der Teigrolle den Augenblick walzen.
Und die Zusammenhänge wieder auftrennen.
   Weil ... wegen ... als ... damit ... um ...
     Vergleiche und ähnliche Alleskleber.
Diese Geschichte muß aufhören.
Mit einem Doppelpunkt schließen:
Ich komme wieder. Ich komme wieder.
Im Vakuum heiter bleiben.
Nur Eigenes stehlen.
Das Chaos
   in verbesserter Ausführung.
     Nicht schmücken – schreiben:

Be stupid, always want to begin from scratch.
Please remind me as soon as I say
hay fever or the Corso of Flowers in Zoppot.
Retrospectively look out of the window.
Rhymes for snipes' droppings.
Loudly join in when anyone's talking nonsense.
Urbin, that's it! – Urbin, that's it!
Hit on the imprecise thing precisely.
Pockets
    are full of old admission tickets.
        Where is the car key?
Delete the car key.
Compassion with verbs.
Believe in the eraser.
Conjure an umbrella in the Lost and Found.
Bulldoze the moment with the rolling pin.
And take the connections apart again.
    Because . . . due to . . . when . . . so that . . . to . . .
        comparisons and similar adhesive aids.
This story must come to an end.
Conclude with a colon:
I'm coming back. I'm coming back.
Remain cheerful in a vacuum.
Steal only things of one's own.
Chaos
    more skilfully executed.
        Not adorn – write:

Die Peitsche

Weil jeder Leiche etwas entsprießt,
weil keine Haut dicht
und kein Geheimnis niet- oder nagelfest ist,
fängt langsam an wie das Gold
der Frühling unter dem Schnee.

Noch schläft die Peitsche und in der Peitsche
aufgerollt der April.
Noch sägt jemand Holz, denkt dabei an den Winter;
und eine Frau geht vorbei,
doch er dreht sich nicht um.

Ein Junge steht auf dem Hof,
schielt und hält eine Peitsche.
Dann dreht er sich langsam, dreht
und schielt nicht mehr, nein er dreht
und knallt haushoch mit der Peitsche.

The Whip

Because something sprouts from every corpse,
because no skin is airtight
and no secret is burglarproof,
slow as gold
spring begins under the snow.

Still the whip sleeps and in the whip
April, rolled up.
Still someone saws logs, thinking of winter,
and a woman passes,
but he doesn't turn his head.

A boy stands in the yard,
squints and holds a whip.
Then he slowly turns, turns around
and no longer squints, no, he turns
and house-high cracks his whip.

Der Dampfkessel-Effekt

Immer zum Zischen bereit.
Schneller gezischt als gedacht.
Nicht mehr mit Fäusten,
zischend wird argumentiert.
Bald wird es heißen:
Er wurde zu Tode gezischt.
Aber noch lebt er und spricht.
Auf seine Frage gab Zischen Antwort.
Seht dieses Volk, im Zischen geeint.
Zischoman. Zischoplex. Zischophil.
Denn das Zischen macht gleich,
kostet wenig und wärmt.
Aber es kostete wessen Geld,
diese Elite, geistreich und zischend,
heranzubilden.
Als wollte Dampfablassen
den nächstliegenden Nero bewegen,
jeweils den Daumen zu senken.
Pfeifen ist schön. Nicht jeder kann pfeifen.
Dieses jedoch, anonym,
macht ängstlich und lässt befürchten ...

The Steam Boiler Effect

Always ready to hiss.
Sooner hissed than thought.
No longer with fists
people argue, but hissing.
Soon they will say:
He was hissed to death.
But still he's alive and speaks.
His questions were answered by hisses.
Look at this people, united in hissing.
Hissomaniac. Hissoplex. Hissophile.
For hissing is a leveller,
costs little and keeps warm.
But it costs whose money
to train
this élite, witty and hissing.
As though letting off steam
could move the local Nero
to the thumb-down sign every time.
Whistling is fine. Not anyone can whistle.
But this thing, anonymous,
is worrying and makes one fear...

In Ohnmacht gefallen

Wir lesen Napalm und stellen Napalm uns vor.
Da wir uns Napalm nicht vorstellen können,
lesen wir über Napalm, bis wir uns mehr
unter Napalm vorstellen können.
Jetzt protestieren wir gegen Napalm.
   Nach dem Frühstück, stumm,
     auf Fotos sehen wir, was Napalm vermag.
   Wir zeigen uns grobe Raster
   und sagen: Siehst du, Napalm.
   Das machen sie mit Napalm.
Bald wird es preiswerte Bildbände
mit besseren Fotos geben,
auf denen deutlicher wird,
was Napalm vermag.
Wir kauen Nägel und schreiben Proteste.
   Aber es gibt, so lesen wir,
   Schlimmeres als Napalm.
   Schnell protestieren wir gegen Schlimmeres.
   Unsere berechtigten Proteste, die wir jederzeit
   verfassen falten frankieren dürfen, schlagen zu Buch.
Ohnmacht, an Gummifassaden erprobt.
Ohnmacht legt Platten auf: ohnmächtige Songs.
Ohne Macht mit Guitarre. –
Aber feinmaschig und gelassen
wirkt sich draussen die Macht aus.

Powerless, with a Guitar

We read napalm and imagine napalm.
Since we cannot imagine napalm
we read about napalm until
by napalm we can imagine more.
Now we protest against napalm.
    After breakfast, silent,
    we see in photographs what napalm can do.
    We show each other coarse screen prints
    and say: there you are, napalm.
    They do that with napalm.
Soon there'll be cheap picture books
with better photographs
which will show more clearly
what napalm can do.
We bite our nails and write protests.
    But, we read, there are
    worse things than napalm.
    Quickly we protest against worse things.
    Our well-founded protests, which at any time
    we may compose fold stamp, mount up.
Impotence, tried out on rubber façades.
Impotence puts records on: impotent songs.
Powerless, with a guitar. –
But outside, finely meshed
and composed, power has its way.

Irgendwas machen

Da können wir doch nicht zusehen.
Wenn wir auch nichts verhindern,
wir müssen uns deutlich machen.
(Mach doch was. Mach doch was.
Irgendwas. Mach doch was.)
Zorn, Ärger und Wut suchten sich ihre Adjektive.
Der Zorn nannte sich gerecht.
Bald sprach man vom alltäglichen Ärger.
Die Wut fiel in Ohnmacht: ohnmächtige Wut.
Ich spreche vom Protestgedicht
und gegen das Protestgedicht.
(Einmal sah ich Rekruten beim Eid
mit Kreuzfingern hinterrücks abschwören.)
Ohnmächtig protestiere ich gegen ohnmächtige Proteste.
Es handelt sich um Oster-, Schweige- und Friedensmärsche.
Es handelt sich um die hundert guten Namen
unter sieben richtigen Sätzen.
Es handelt sich um Guitarren und ähnliche
die Schallplatte fördernde Protestinstrumente.
Ich rede vom hölzernen Schwert und vom fehlenden Zahn,
vom Protestgedicht.

Wie Stahl seine Konjunktur hat, hat Lyrik ihre Konjunktur.
Aufrüstung öffnet Märkte für Antikriegsgedichte.
Die Herstellungskosten sind gering.
Man nehme: ein Achtel gerechten Zorn,
zwei Achtel alltäglichen Ärger
und fünf Achtel, damit sie vorschmeckt, ohnmächtige Wut.
Denn mittelgrosse Gefühle gegen den Krieg
sing billig zu haben

Do Something

We can't just look on.
Even if we can't stop anything
we must say what we think.
(Do something. Do something.
Anything. Do something, then.)
Indignation, annoyance, rage looked for their adjectives.
Indignation called itself righteous.
Soon people spoke of everyday annoyance.
Rage fell into impotence: impotent rage.
I speak of the protest poem
and against the protest poem.
(Once I saw recruits taking the oath
unswear it behind their backs with crossed fingers.)
Impotently I protest against impotent protests.
What I mean is Easter, silence and peace marches.
What I mean is the hundred good names
underneath seven true sentences.
What I mean is guitars and similar
protest instruments conducive to records.
I speak of the wooden sword and the missing tooth,
of the protest poem.

Just as steel has its booms, so poetry has its booms.
Rearmament opens markets for anti-war poems.
The cost of production is low.
Take an eighth of righteous indignation,
two eighths of everyday annoyance
and five eighths – to heighten that flavour – of impotent rage.
For medium-sized feelings against the war
are cheaply obtained

und seit Troja schon Ladenhüter.
(Mach doch was. Mach doch was.
Irgenwas. Mach doch was.)

Man macht sich Luft: schon verraucht der gerechte Zorn.
Der kleine alltägliche Ärger lässt die Ventile zischen.
Ohnmächtige Wut entlädt sich, füllt einen Luftballon,
der steigt und steigt, wird kleiner und kleiner, ist weg.
Sind Gedichte Atemübungen?
Wenn sie diesen Zweck erfüllen, – und ich frage,
prosaisch wie mein Grossvater, nach dem Zweck, –
dann ist Lyrik Therapie.
Ist das Gedicht eine Waffe?
Manche, überarmiert, können kaum laufen.
Sie müssen das Unbehagen an Zuständen
als Vehikel benutzen:
sie kommen ans Ziel, sie kommen ans Ziel:
zuerst ins Feuilleton und dann in die Anthologie:
Die Napalm-Metapher und ihre Abwandlungen
im Protestgedicht der sechziger Jahre.
Es handelt sich um Traktatgedichte.
Gerechter Zorn zählt Elend und Terror auf.
Alltäglicher Ärger findet den Reim auf fehlendes Brot.
Ohnmächtige Wut macht atemlos von sich reden.
(Mach doch was. Mach doch was . . .)
Dabei gibt es Hebelgesetze.
Sie aber kreiden ihm an, dem Stein,
er wolle sich nicht bewegen.
Tags drauf ködert der hilflose Stil berechtigter Proteste
den treffsicheren Stil glatter Dementis.
Weil sie in der Sache zwar jeweils recht haben,
sich im Detail aber allzu leicht irren,
distanzieren sich die Unterzeichner

and have been shopsoiled ever since Troy.
(Do something. Do something.
Anything. Do something, then.)

One lets off steam: already righteous indignation goes up in
   smoke.
The small everyday annoyance makes the safety valves hiss.
Impotent rage discharges itself, fills a balloon with gas,
this rises, rises, grows smaller and smaller, is gone.
Are poems breathing exercises?
If that is their function – and prosaic
as my grandfather, I ask what their function is –
then poetry is therapy.
Is a poem a weapon?
Some, too heavily armed, can hardly walk.
They have to use their dissatisfaction with circumstances
as a vehicle:
they reach their destination, they can hit the mark:
first the weekly paper, then the anthology:
the napalm metaphor and its permutations
in the protest poem of the sixties.
I mean poems that are tracts.
Righteous indignation enumerates terrors and miseries.
Everyday annoyance discovers the rhyme for no bread.
Impotent rage sets people talking breathlessly about itself.
(Do something. Do something . . .)
There are laws of leverage.
But they hold it against the stone
that it will not budge.
Next day the helpless style of well-founded protest
acts as a bait for the well-aimed style of smooth refutation.
Since in the cause they are always right
but all too easily slip up over details

halblaut von den Verfassern und ihren Protesten.
(Nicht nur Diebe kaufen sich Handschuhe.)
Was übrig bleibt: zählebige Missverständnisse
zitieren einander. Fehlerhafte Berichtigungen
lernen vom Meerschweinchen
und vermehren sich unübersichtlich.

Da erbarmt sich der Stein und tut so,
als habe man ihn verrückt:
während Zorn, Ärger und Wut einander ins Wort fallen,
treten die Spezialisten der Macht
lächelnd vor Publikum auf. Sie halten fundierte Vorträge
über den Preis, den die Freiheit fordert;
über Napalm und seine abschreckende Wirkung;
über berechtigte Proteste und die erklärliche Wut.
Das alles ist erlaubt.
Da die Macht nur die Macht achtet,
darf solange ohnmächtig protestiert werden,
bis nicht mehr, weil der Lärm stört,
protestiert werden darf. –
Wir aber verachten die Macht.
Wir sind nicht mächtig, beteuern wir uns.
Ohne Macht gefallen wir uns in Ohnmacht.
Wir wollen die Macht nicht; sie aber hat uns. –
Nun fühlt sich der gerechte Zorn mißverstanden.
Der alltägliche Ärger mündet in Schweigemärsche,
die zuvor angemeldet und genehmigt wurden.
Im Kreis läuft die ohnmächtige Wut.
Das fördert den gleichfalls gerechten Zorn
verärgerter Polizisten:
ohnmächtige Wut wird handgreiflich.
Die Faust wächst sich zum Kopf aus
und denkt in Tiefschlägen Leberhaken knöchelhart.

the signatories tacitly half-dissociate themselves
from the authors and from their protests.
(Not only burglars buy gloves.)
What remains is: resilient misunderstandings
quote one another. Erroneous corrections
learn from guinea pigs
how to breed so that no one keeps track.

The stone takes pity and acts
as though it had been moved:
while indignation, annoyance and rage interrupt one
    another,
the specialists in power
appear smiling in front of the public. They make well-
    informed speeches
about the price demanded for freedom:
about napalm and its deterrent effects;
about well-founded protests and understandable rage.
All this is permitted.
Since power respects only power
impotent protest is allowed to carry on
until, because the noise is disturbing,
protest is no longer allowed. –
But we despise power.
We are not powerful, we keep assuring each other.
Without power we enjoy our impotence.
We do not want power; but power has us. –
Now righteous indignation feels misunderstood.
Our everyday annoyance ends in silence marches
that have first been announced and permitted.
Our impotent rage runs around in circles.
This provokes the equally righteous indignation
of angered policemen:

(Mach doch was. Mach doch was . . .)
Das alles macht Schule und wird von der Macht
gestreichelt geschlagen subventioniert.
Schon setzt der Stein, der bewegt werden wollte,
unbewegt Moos an.
Geht das so weiter? – Im Kreis schon.
Was sollen wir machen? – Nicht irgendwas.
Wohin mit der Wut? – Ich weiss ein Rezept:

Schlagt in die Schallmauer Nägel.
Köpft Pusteblumen und Kerzen.
Setzt auf dem Sofa euch durch.
   Wir haben immer noch Wut.
   Schon sind wir überall heiser.
   Wir sind gegen alles umsonst.
   Was sollen wir jetzt noch machen?
   Wo sollen wir hin mit der Wut?
Mach doch was. Mach doch was.
Wir müssen irgendwas,
mach doch was, machen.
   Los, protestieren wir schnell.
   Der will nicht mitprotestieren.
   Los, unterschreib schon und schnell.
   Du warst doch immer dagegen.
   Wer nicht unterschreibt, ist dafür.
Schön ist die Wut im Gehege,
bevor sie gefüttert wird.
Lang lief die Ohnmacht im Regen,
die Strümpfe trocknet sie jetzt.
Wut und Ventile, darüber Gesang:
Ohnmacht, dein Nadelöhr ist der Gesang:
   Weil ich nichts machen kann,
   weil ich nichts machen kann,

impotent rage becomes aggressive.
The fist grows into a head
and thinks in terms of low blows hooks to the liver knuckle-
     hard.
(Do something. Do something . . .)
All this becomes institutionalized, and by power
is caressed beaten subsidized.
Already the stone that was to be moved
gathers moss, unmoved.
Can we go on like that? – Yes, in a circle.
What shall we do? – Not anything.
How express our rage? – I know a recipe:

Strike nails into the sound barrier.
Behead dandelions and candles.
Assert yourselves on the couch.
     We still feel rage.
     Already we're hoarse all over.
     We're against everything, vainly.
     What else can we do now?
     How shall we express our rage?
Do something. Do something.
We must do something or other,
do something, do it.
     Come on, then, quickly protest.
     That fellow won't join our protest.
     Come on, then, quickly sign.
     You've always been against it.
     Those who don't sign are for it.
Lovely is rage in the paddock,
before it is fed.
For a long time impotence ran around in the rain,
but now it is drying its socks.

hab ich die Wut, hab ich die Wut.
Mach doch was. Mach doch was.
Irgendwas. Mach doch was.
Wir müssen irgendwas,
hilft doch nix, hilft doch nix,
wir müssen irgendwas,
mach doch was, machen.
Lauf schweigend Protest.
Lief ich schon. Lief ich schon.
Schreib ein Gedicht.
Hab ich schon. Hab ich schon.
Koch eine Sülze. Schweinekopfsülze:
die Ohnmacht geliere, die Wut zittre nach.
Ich weiss ein Rezept; wer kocht es mir nach?

Rage and safety valves, about them a song;
Impotence, your needle's eye is a song.
   Because I can't do anything,
   because I can't do anything
   I'm full of rage, I'm full of rage.
   Do something, then. Do something.
   Anything. Do something, then.
   We must do something or other,
   does no good, does no good,
   we must do something or other,
   do something, do it.
Silently march in protest.
Have done it once, have done it.
Write a poem, then.
Have written it, have done it.
Cook some brawn. Pig's head brawn:
let impotence jell, rage quiver in sympathy.
I know a recipe; who'll follow it cooking?

Die Schweinekopfsülze

Man nehme: einen halben Schweinekopf
samt Ohr und Fettbacke,
lasse die halbierte Schnauze, den Ohransatz,
die Hirnschale und das Jochbein anhacken,
lege alles mit zwei gespaltenen Spitzbeinen,
denen zuvor die blaue Schlachthofmarkierung
entfernt werden sollte,
mit nelkengespickter Zwiebel, grossem Lorbeerblatt,
mit einer Kinderhand Senfkörner
und einem gestrichenen Suppenlöffel mittlere Wut
in kochendes Salzwasser,
wobei darauf zu achten ist,
dass in geräumigem Topf alle Teile
knapp mit Wasser bedeckt sind,
und der Ohrlappen, weil er sonst ansetzt,
nicht flach auf den Topfboden gedrückt wird.
  Fünf viertel Stunden lasse man kochen,
  wobei es ratsam ist, nach dem ersten Aufkochen
  mit der Schaumkelle
  die sämigen, braungrauen Absonderungen
  der inneren Schnauzenteile, sowie der Ohrmuschel
  und der halbierten leeren Hirnschale
  abzuschöpfen, damit wir zu einer klaren,
  wenn auch geschmacksärmeren Sülze kommen,
  zumal sich die rasch zum Protest gerinnende Wut,
  wie jede ohnmächtige, also eiweisshaltige Leidenschaft,
  wenn sie nicht rasch gleichmässig unterrührt wird,
  gern in weissen Partikeln dem Schaum mitteilt.
Inzwischen wiege man vier Zwiebeln
und zwei geschälte

The Jellied Pig's Head

Take half a pig's head
including ear and cheek,
have the halved snout, the root of the ear,
the brainpan and the cheekbone chined,
together with two split trotters
from which the blue inspection stamp
should first have been removed,
with a clove-studded onion, a large bay leaf,
with a child's handful of mustard seed
and a level tablespoon of medium rage
place them all in boiling salt water,
taking care
that in the large pot every part
is barely covered with water
and the flap of the ear, which otherwise would stick,
is not pressed down flat on to the bottom.
    Boil gently for an hour and a quarter,
    remembering that after the first boiling-up
    it is advisable to scoop off with a ladle
    the frothy brownish-grey excretions
    from the inner part of the snout, the conch of the ear
    and the halved, empty brainpan,
    so as to obtain a pure
    though not very savoury brawn,
    particularly as the rage, which so easily curdles to protest,
    tends to communicate in white particles with the froth
    unless constantly stirred from the start.
Meanwhile chop up four onions
and two peeled
and cored apples,

und vom Gehäuse befreite Äpfel
möglichst klein,
schneide zwei Salzgurken, –
niemals Dill-, Senf- oder Delikatessgurken, –
zu winzigen Würfeln,
zerstosse in Gedanken wie im Mörser
eine gefüllte Schlüsselbeinkuhle sohwarzen Pfeffer
und lasse die restliche Wut
mit beigelegter Ingwerwurzel
und wenig geriebener Zitronenschale
auf kleiner Flamme ohnmächtig ziehen.
      Sobald, – nach einer Stichprobe in die Fettbacke, –
      das Kopffleisch weich ist,
      die Backenzähne im Zahnbett gelockert sind,
      aber noch haften,
      und sich die besonders geleespendenden Hautteile
      vom Ohr und an den Spalträndern
      der beigelegten Spitzbeine zu lösen beginnen,
      nehme man alle Teile,
      sowie die nelkengespickte Zwiebel
      und das Lorbeerblatt aus dem Topf,
      suche mit der Schaumkelle den Topfboden
      nach Knochensplittern
      und den sich leicht lösenden Vorderzähnen,
      sowie nach dem kiesig knirschenden Sand
      der Ohrmuschel ab und lasse, während der Sud
      auf kleingestelltem Feuer weiterziehen sollte,
      alles auf einer Platte,
      möglichst bei offenem Küchenfenster
      und verengten Pupillen, abkühlen.
Jetzt gilt es, die Weichteile der Schnauze,
die Fettbacke samt eingebettetem Auge
und das darunter gelagerte Fleisch

preferably small,
cut up two salted gherkins –
never dill, mustard or vinegar pickled gherkins –
into tiny cubes,
pound in your mind as though in a mortar
a heaped collarbone pit of black pepper
and, adding a ginger root,
as well as a little grated lemon peel,
leave the remaining rage
to simmer impotently over a low flame.
 As soon as – after a trial jab at the cheek –
 the meat of the head is tender,
 the back teeth are loose in the gums
 but still rooted,
 and the most jelly-conducive parts of the skin
 around the ear and the split edges
 of the added trotters begin to peel off,
 take all the components
 as well as the clove-studded onion
 and the bay leaf out of the pot,
 search the bottom with your ladle
 for bone splinters
 and the easily loosening front teeth,
 also for the grit-like grinding sand
 of the ear conch, and leave it all to cool
 on a platter,
 preferably with the kitchen windows open
 and the pupils of your eyes contracted,
 while the broth should be left to simmer
 over a low flame.
Now proceed to detach
the soft parts of the snout,
the cheek, including the eye embedded in it,

von den Knochen zu lösen.
    Es sie angeraten, auf weiche
    bis schnittfeste Knorpelteile,
    sowie auf den gallertartigen Ohrbelag,
    der sich mit dem Messerrücken leichthin
    vom eigentlichen Ohrlappen schaben lässt,
    nicht zu verzichten,
    weil gerade diese Teile,
    desgleichen das lamellenförmige Zahnfleisch
    und der hornige,
    zur Speise- und Luftröhre leitende Zungenansatz,
    unserer Sülze den speziellen
    und leidenschaftlichen Sülzgeschmack geben.
Auch scheue man sich nicht,
die während der Arbeit immer wieder rasch
von einem Geleefilm überzogenen Hände
über dem dampfenden Sud abtropfen zu lassen,
weil so der Prozess des natürlichen Gelierens
abermals unterstützt wird;
denn unsere Schweinekopfsülze
soll ganz aus sich und mitgeteilter Wut,
also ohne Macht und Gelantinepapier steif werden.
    Alsdann würfle man das
    von den Knochen gelöste Fett und Fleisch,
    desgleichen die Knorpel und Weichteile,
    lege sie mit den gewiegten Zwiebeln und Äpfeln,
    den winziggewürfelten Gurken,
    dem gestossenen Schwarzpfeffer
    und einem satten Griff Kapern in den Sud.
Mit, – nach Geschmack, –
löffelweis unterrührtem Estragonessig, –
es wird empfohlen, kräftig zu säuern,
weil Essig kalt gerne nachgibt, –

and the layers of flesh beneath them,
from the bones.
    We recommend that you do not
    leave out the soft
    and firmer gristle
    or the jelly-like covering of the ear
    that can easily be scraped off with the back of a knife
    from the ear flap proper,
    since those very parts,
    like the lamellated gums
    and the horny
    root of the tongue that leads to windpipe and oesophagus
    impart to our brawn
    that special and passionate brawn flavour.
Also, you should not fail
to let your hands, which during your work
have been covered again and again
with a film of jelly, drip dry
over the steaming broth,
because in that way the process of natural jelling
is aided once more;
for our jellied pig's head is to set
all by itself and communicated rage,
that is, without power and gelatine paper.
    Then cut up the fat and meat
    detached from the bones, not omitting the gristle,
    and together with the chopped onions and apples,
    the minutely cubed gherkins,
    the pounded black pepper,
    and an ample pinch of capers, place them in the broth.
Together with tarragon vinegar,
stirred in by the spoonful, according to taste –
we recommend a not too sparing use

lasse man alles noch einmal aufkochen,
gebe jetzt erst,
nach wenig Bedenken,
die mittlerweile
auf kleiner Flamme
schön eingedickte Wut
ohne die ausgelaugte Ingwerwurzel bei
und fülle alsdann eine zuvor
mit kaltem Wasser geschwenkte Steingutschüssel.
    Diese stelle man an einen kühlen,
    wenn möglich zugigen Ort
    und lade sich für den nächsten Abend
    freundliche Gäste ins Haus,
    die eine hausgemachte Schweinekopfsülze
    zu schätzen wissen.
Sparsamer Nachsatz: Wer ungern etwas verkommen lässt,
der lasse Grossknorpel und Knochen,
sowie die gespaltenen Spitzbeine
noch einmal auskochen,
verfeinere mit Majoran, Mohrrüben, Sellerie,
gebe, falls immer noch restliche Wut im Hause,
eine Messerspitze dazu
und gweinne so eine schmackhafte Suppe,
die, wenn man Wruken, Graupen, sonstige Kümmernisse
oder geschälte Erbsen beilegt,
kinderreichen Familien ein zwar einfaches,
aber nahrhaftes Essen zu ersetzen vermag.

because vinegar tends to weaken when cold –
bring it all to the boil once more,
only now, after brief hesitation,
adding the rage
which meanwhile
has well thickened
over a low flame,
without the drained ginger root,
and then proceed to fill
a stoneware dish previously rinsed with cold water.
    Place this in a cool,
    if possibly draughty place
    and for the next night
    invite well-disposed guests
    who will appreciate
    a home-made pig's head brawn.
Thrifty postscriptum: people who don't like waste
should cook the coarse gristle and bones
as well as the split trotters
once again, for spice
adding marjoram, celery, carrots
and, provided more rage remains in the house,
a knife-tip of that,
so gaining a tasty soup
which, with turnips, barley, similar miseries
or dried peas
can replace for families with many children
a simple but nutritious meal.

Liebe Geprüft

Dein Apfel – mein Apfel.
Jetzt beißen wir gleichzeitig zu:
schau, wie auf ewig verschieden.
Jetzt legen wir Apfel und Apfel
Biß gegen Biß.

Love Tested

Your apple – my apple.
Now we bite at the same time:
look, how forever differently.
Now we lay apple to apple
bite beside bite.

Dein Ohr

Gutzureden wahrsagen.
Wollte mich ausgesprochen versenken.
Wollte verstanden sein dumm.
Nur zwischen Gänsefüßchen oder gedruckt
bleigefaßt lügen.

Was keinen Grund findet aber Antwort bekommt:
logische Ketten,
geständiges Flüstern,
die Pause ausgespart,
Sprachschotter Lautgeröll.

In den Wind gehißt,
flattert dein Ohr,
hört sich flattern.

Beim Fädeln spleißen die Wörter danebengesagt.

Your Ear

Soothingly reassure. Blandly tell fortune.
Wished to communicate deeply.
For my stupidity wanted your understanding.
Between quotation marks only or printed,
set in lead, to lie.

What finds no reason but receives an answer:
logical chains,
confessional whispering,
the interval kept in reserve,
speech-rubble sound-scree.

Hoisted into the wind
Your ear flutters,
hears itself flutter.

As I thread words they split, spoken off-target.

Gestillt

Die Brust meiner Mutter war groß und weiß.
Den Zitzen anliegen.
Schmarotzen, bevor sie Flasche und Nuckel wird.
Mit Stottern, Komplexen drohen,
wenn sie versagt werden sollte.
Nicht nur quengeln.

Klare Fleischbrühe läßt die Milch einschießen
oder Sud aus Dorschköpfen trüb gekocht,
bis Fischaugen blind
ungefähr Richtung Glück rollen.

Männer nähren nicht.
Männer schielen heimwärts wenn Kühe
mit schwerem Euter die Straße
und den Berufsverkehr sperren.
Männer träumen die dritte Brust.
Männer neiden dem Säugling.
und immer fehlt ihnen.

Unsere bärtigen Brustkinder,
die uns steuerpflichtig versorgen,
schmatzen in Pausen zwischen Terminen,
an Zigaretten gelehnt.

Ab vierzig sollten alle Männer wieder gesäugt werden:
öffentlich und gegen Gebühr,
bis sie ohne Wunsch satt sind und nicht mehr weinen,
auf dem Klo weinen müssen: allein.

Comforted

My mother's breast was big and white.
Snuggle up to the teats.
Batten, before it turns into bottle and rubber.
Threaten a stammer, complexes,
if it should be withheld.
Whining is not enough.

A clear meat broth lets the milk jet in
or a stock of cods' heads boiled till it's murky
until fish eyes, blind,
roll off in the vague direction of bliss.

Men do not nourish.
Men squint homeward when cows
with heavy udders obstruct
the road and rush-hour traffic.
Men dream of the third breast.
Men envy the suckling infant
and always feel deprived.

Our bearded breast-fed babies
who, taxable, earn our keep,
smack their lips in lulls between engagements
while they lean on cigarettes.

After forty all men should be suckled again:
publicly, at a fixed price,
till they are comforted, wishless, and needn't cry any more,
cry in the john, alone.

Wie Ich mich sehe

Spiegelverkehrt und deutlicher schief.
Schon überlappen die oberen Lider.
Das eine Auge hängt müde, verschlagen das andere wach.
Soviel Einsicht und Innerei,
nachdem ich laut wiederholt
die Macht und ihren Besitz verbellt habe.
(Wir werden! Es wird! Das muß!)

Seht die porigen Backen.
Noch oder wieder: Federn blase ich leicht
und behaupte, was schwebt.
Wissen möchte das Kinn, wann es zittern darf endlich.
Dicht hält die Stirn; dem Ganzen fehlt ein Gedanke.
Wo, wenn das Ohr verdeckt ist
oder an andere Bilder verliehen,
nistet in Krümeln Gelächter?

Alles verschattet und mit Erfahrung verhängt.
Die Brille habe ich seitlich gelegt.
Nur aus Gewohnheit wittert die Nase.
Den Lippen,
die immer noch Federn blasen,
lese ich Durst ab.

Unterm Euter der schwarzweißen Kuh:
ich sehe mich trinken
oder dir angelegt, Köchin,
nachdem deine Brust
tropfend über dem garenden Fisch hing;
du findest mich schön.

How I See Myself

Mirror-inverted and more clearly awry.
Already the upper eyelids overlap.
One eye hangs weary, the other cunning, alert.
So much insight and inwardness, after aloud
repeatedly I had barked at power and its possessions.
(We shall! It will! It must!)

Look at those porous cheeks.
Still or again, feathers I blow with ease
and assert that which hovers.
The chin wants to know when at last it may tremble.
It's the forehead that holds you together, the whole lacks a
    thought.
Where, when the ear is covered
or lent to other pictures,
does laughter nestle in crumbs?

Everything overshadowed and veiled with experience.
I have tilted the spectacles to one side.
Only from habit the nose catches a scent.
From the lips
that blow feathers still
I read thirst.

Under the black and white cow's udder:
I see myself drink
or sucking from you, cook,
after your breast
had hung dripping over the boiling fish;
you think me handsome.

Sargnägel

Woran ich mich halte,
wovon ich nicht lasse,
was an der Lippe mir hängt,
weshalb ich mit Rauchzeichen
mich beweise: Seht!

Noch lebt es, kringelt sich,
speichert Rückstände,
hält seinen Traum wach
und will sich verbrauchen,
wie da geschrieben steht
und aus Asche zu lesen ist:
Worte am Kreuz.

Seine Sargnägel (sieben)
aus anderer Zeitweil,
handgeschmiedet und kürzlich wiedergefunden,
als der Friedhof nahbei, weil außer Betrieb
(und neuzugewinnender Parkplätze wegen),
gründlich planiert wurde.

Deshalb rauche ich
gegen jede Vernunft.

Coffin Nails

That to which I cling,
that I never cease from,
that which hangs on my lips,
that for which with smoke signals
I prove myself: look!

Still it's alive, still curls,
stores up arrears,
keeps its dream awake
and wants to use itself up
as it is written
and to be read from ashes:
words on the cross.

His coffin nails (seven)
from a different provisional era,
handmade and found again lately,
when the nearby graveyard, because out of use
(and for the sake of new parking lots),
was thoroughly bulldozed.

That's why I smoke
in the teeth of all reason.

Müll unser

Suchte Steine und fand
den überlebenden Handschuh
aus synthetischer Masse.

Jeder Fingerling sprach
Nein, nicht die dummen Seglergeschichten,
sondern was bleiben wird:

Müll unser
Strände lang.
Während abhanden wir
niemand Verlust sein werden.

Our Litter Which

Looked for pebbles and found
the surviving glove
made of synthetic pulp.

Every finger spoke.
No, not those daft yachtsman's yarns
but of what will remain:

our litter
beaches long.
While we, mislaid,
will be nobody's loss.

Abschied nehmen

Mir träumte, ich müßte Abschied nehmen
von allen Dingen, die mich umstellt haben
und ihren Schatten werfen: die vielen besitzanzeigenden
Fürwörter. Abschied vom Inventar, dieser Liste
diverser Fundsachen. Abschied
von den ermüdenden Düften,
den Gerüchen, mich wachzuhalten, von der Süße,
der Bitternis, vom Sauren an sich
und von der hitzigen Schärfe des Pfefferkorns.
Abschied vom Ticktack der Zeit, vom Ärger am Montag,
dem schäbigen Mittwochsgewinn, vom Sonntag
und dessen Tücke, sobald Langeweile Platz nimmt.
Abschied von allen Terminen: was zukünftig
fällig sein soll.

Mir träumte, ich müßte von jeder Idee, ob tot
oder lebend geboren, vom Sinn, der den Sinn
hinterm Sinn sucht,
und von der Dauerläuferin Hoffnung auch
mich verabschieden. Abschied vom Zinseszins
der gesparten Wut, vom Erlös gespeicherter Träume,
von allem, was auf Papier steht, erinnert zum Gleichnis,
als Roß und Reiter Denkmal wurde. Abschied
von allen Bildern, die sich der Mensch gemacht hat.
Abschied vom Lied, dem gereimten Jammer, Abschied
von den geflochtenen Stimmen, vom Jubel sechschörig,
dem Eifer der Instrumente,
von Gott und Bach.

Leavetaking

I dreamed that I must take leave
of all the things that surrounded me
and cast their shadows: all those possessive
pronouns. And of the inventory, list
of diverse things found. Take leave
of the wearying odours,
smells, to keep me awake, of sweetness,
of bitterness, of sourness per se
and the peppercorn's fiery sharpness.
Take leave of time's ticktock, of Monday's annoyance,
Wednesday's shabby gains, of Sunday
and its treacheries, as soon as boredom sits down.
Take leave of all deadlines: of what in the future
is to be due.

I dreamed that of every idea, whether stillborn
or live, of the sense that looks
for the sense behind sense,
and of the long-distance runner hope as well
I must take leave. Take leave of the compound interest,
of saved-up fury, the proceeds of stored dreams,
of all that's written on paper, recalled as analogy
when horse and rider became a memorial. Take leave
of all the images men have made for themselves.
Take leave of the song, rhymed bellyaching, and of
voices that interweave, that six-part jubilation,
the fervour of instruments,
of God and of Bach.

Mir träumte, ich müßte Abschied nehmen
vom kahlen Geäst,
von den Wörtern Knospe, Blüte und Frucht,
von den Zeiten des Jahres, die ihre Stimmungen
satt haben und auf Abschied bestehen.
Frühnebel. Spätsommer. Wintermantel. April April! rufen,
noch einmal Herbstzeitlos und Märzbecher sagen,
Dürre Frost Schmelze.
Den Spuren im Schnee davonlaufen. Vielleicht
sind zum Abschied die Kirschen reif. Vielleicht
spielt der Kuckuck verrückt und ruft. Noch einmal
Erbsen aus Schoten grün springen lassen. Oder
die Pusteblume: jetzt erst begreife ich, was sie will.

Ich träumte, ich müßte von Tisch, Tür und Bett
Abschied nehmen und den Tisch, die Tür und das Bett
belasten, weit öffnen, zum Abschied erproben.
Mein letzter Schultag: ich buchstabiere die Namen
der Freunde und sage ihre Telefonnummern auf: Schulden
sind zu begleichen; ich schreibe zum Schluß meinen Feinden
ein Wort: Schwamm drüber – oder:
Es lohnte den Streit nicht.
Auf einmal habe ich Zeit.
Es sucht mein Auge, als sei es geschult worden,
Abschied zu nehmen, rundum Horizonte, die Hügel
hinter den Hügeln, die Stadt
auf beiden Seiten des Flusses ab,
als müßte erinnert verschont gerettet werden, was
auf der Hand liegt: zwar aufgegeben, doch immer noch
dinglich, hellwach.

Mir träumte, ich müßte Abschied nehmen
von dir, dir und dir, von meinem Ungenügen,

I dreamed that I must take leave
of bare branchwork,
of the words bud, blossom and fruit,
of the seasons that, sick of their moods,
insist on departure.
Early mist, late summer. Winter coat. Call out: April April!
say again autumn crocus and may tree,
drought frost thaw.
Run away from tracks in the snow. Perhaps
when I go the cherries will be ripe. Perhaps
the cuckoo will act mad and call. Once more
let peas jump green from their pods. Or the
dandelion clock: only now do I grasp what it wants.

I dreamed that of table, door and bed
I must take leave and put a strain on
table, door and bed, open them wide, test them in going.
My last schoolday: I spell out the names
of my friends and recite their telephone numbers: debts
are to be settled: last of all I write to my enemies
briefly: let bygones be bygones – or:
It wasn't worth quarrelling over.
Suddenly I have time.
My eyes as though they'd been trained
in leavetaking, search horizons all around, the hills
behind the hills, the city
on either bank of the river,
as though what goes without saying
must be remembered preserved saved: given up, true, but still
palpable, wide-awake.

I dreamed that I must take leave
of you, you and you, of my insufficiency,

dem restlichen Ich: was hinterm Komma blieb
und kümmert seit Jahren.
Abschied von sattsam vertrauter Fremde,
von den Gewohnheiten, die sich Recht geben höflich,
von unserem eingeschrieben verbrieften Haß. Nichts
war mir näher als deine Kälte. So viel Liebe genau
falsch erinnert. Am Ende
war alles versorgt: Sicherheitsnadeln zuhauf.
Bleibt noch der Abschied von deinen Geschichten,
die immer das Bollwerk, den Dampfer suchen,
der von Stralsund, aus der brennenden Stadt
beladen mit Flüchtlingen kommt;
und Abschied von meinen Gläsern, die Scherben, allzeit
nur Scherben, sich selbst als Scherben
im Sinn hatten. Nein,
keine Kopfstände mehr.

Und nie wieder Schmerz. Nichts,
dem Erwartung entgegenliefe. Dieses Ende
ist Schulstoff, bekannt. Dieser Abschied
wurde in Kursen geübt. Seht nur, wie billig
Geheimnisse nackt sind! Kein Geld zahlt Verrat mehr aus.
Zu Schleuderpreisen des Feindes entschlüsselte Träume.
Endlich hebt sich der Vorteil auf, macht uns
die Schlußrechnung gleich,
siegt zum letzten Mal die Vernunft,
ist ohne Unterschied alles,
was einen Odem führt, alles, was kreucht
und fleucht, alles, was noch
ungedacht und was werden sollte vielleicht,
am Ende und scheidet aus.

the residual self: what remained behind the comma
and for years has rankled.
Take leave of the familiar strangeness we live with,
of the habits that politely justify themselves,
of the bonded and registered hatred between us. Nothing
was closer to me than your coldness. So much love recalled
with precise wrongness. In the end
everything had been seen to: safety pins galore.
Lastly, the leavetaking from your stories
that always look for the bulwark, the steamer
out of Stralsund, the city on fire,
laden with refugees;
take leave of my glassware that had shards in mind,
only shards at all times, shards
of itself. Not that:
no more headstands.

And no more pain, ever. Nothing
that expectation might run to meet. This end
is classroom stuff, stale. This leavetaking
was crammed for in courses. Just look how cheaply
secrets go naked! Betrayal pays out no more money.
Decoded dreams of the enemy, at cut-rate prices.
At last advantage cancels itself, evens out for us
the balance sheet,
reason triumphs for the last time,
levelling
all that has breath, all things that creep
or fly, all that had not yet
been thought and was to be perhaps,
at an end, on its way out.

Doch als mir träumte, ich müßte
von jeglicher Kreatur, damit von keinem Getier,
dem einst Noah die Arche gezimmert,
Nachgeschmack bliebe, Abschied nehmen sofort,
träumte ich nach dem Fisch, dem Schaf und dem Huhn,
die mit dem Menschengeschlecht alle vergingen,
eine einzelne Ratte mir, die warf neun Junge
und hatte Zukunft für sich.

But when I dreamed that I must
take leave at once of all creation
so that of no animal for which Noah once
built the ark there should be a redolence,
after the fish, the sheep and the hen
that all perished together with humankind,
I dreamed for myself one rat that gave birth to nine
and was blessed with a future.

Das Unsre

Breit liegt das Land, in dessen Lied wie in Prospekten
sich Schönheit weit gehügelt austrägt, gegen Norden flach,
besiedelt, eng (in dieser Zeit) bis unters Dach.
Wo sich die Kinder einst vor Vaters Zorn versteckten,

ist keine Zuflucht mehr, nein, nichts schließt mehr geheim.
So offen sind wir kenntlich, allseits ausgestellt,
daß jeder Nachbar, ringsum alle Welt
als Unglück treiben sieht, was unsres Glückes Keim.

Wo wir uns finden, hat verkehrte Konjunktur
uns fett gemacht. Dank Leid und Kummer satt,
schlug mästend Elend an als freien Marktes Kur;
und selbst auf unsre Sünden gab's Rabatt.
Still liegt Novemberland, verflucht zum tugendhaften Fleiß,
in Angst vorm Jüngstgericht, dem überhöhten Preis.

What's Ours

Broad lies the land whose anthem like its brochure pages
a beauty widely hillocked fills, toward the north more flat,
all peopled, densely (now) up to each attic slat.
Where children used to hide from Father's cruel rages

no refuge now remains, no secret lock in need.
So well we advertise, exhibit with such pride
that every neighbour, all the world outside
sees as disaster's shoot what we call happy seed.

Where now we find ourselves, a specious boom of shares
had fattened us. With grief and suffering sated,
a force-fed misery peddled free-market wares;
and at a discount our worst sins were rated.
Hushed lies Novemberland, condemned to virtuous sweat
for fear of Judgement Day, inflation gross and net.

Novemberland

Da komm ich her. Das feiert jährlich alle Neune.
Von dem ich weg will über selbsterdachte Zäune,
doch in verkehrten Schuhen dahin laufe, wo ich heiße
und ruchbar bin für die zurückgelaßne Scheiße.

Das bleibt veränderlich sich gleich
und ähnelt unterm Schutt der Moden –
mal sind es Jeans, dann wieder Loden –
den abgelebten Fotos aus dem Dritten Reich.

Novembertote, laßt sie ruhn!
Wir haben mit uns Lebenden genug zu tun.
Doch diese sind nicht jene, jene sind erwacht
und haben sich als Täter das gleiche ähnlich ausgedacht.
Nicht abgebucht noch steuerfrei ist der Gewinn
aus Schuldenlast, für die ich haftbar bin.

Novemberland

That's where I'm from. That yearly celebrates every nine.*
That's what I wish to leave, cross fences never mine
but in the wrong shoes run to where I'm part of it
and am responsible for the residuous shit.

That changeably remains the same,
beneath the trash of trends is like –
now blue jeans, now green loden are the name of the game –
faded, discarded photos from our late Third Reich.

November's dead, leave them alone!
For us who live there's quite enough now to be done.
But these are not the others, those have now awoken,
thought up the same as doers by the self-same token.
Not written off nor tax-free is the profit made
from debts that now by my sort must be paid.

*Translator's note: An allusion not only to the game of skittles, in which nine
is the top score, but to Hitler's *putsch* in 1923, the *Kristallnacht* of 1938, and the
end of the Berlin Wall in 1989, all of which occurred on November 9.

Späte Sonnenblumen

November schlug sie, schwarz in schwarz vor Hell.
Noch ragen Strünke, sind der Farben Spott,
im Regen schräg und suchen sich Vergleiche,
auch Reime, etwa Gott und Leiche.

Noch immer tauglich, stehn sie mir Modell,
weil ausgesägt vor Himmeln, deren Grau
im Ausschnitt und total zerfließt,
drauf eine Meldung sich als Botschaft liest:

Geschieden sind wie Mann und Frau
nach kurzer Ehe Land und Leute.
Karg war die Ernte, reich die Beute.
Ach, Treuhand hat uns abgeschöpft.
Wer bei Verdacht schon Sonnenblumen köpft,
dem werden Zeugen fehlen, den erwischt die Meute.

Late Sunflowers

November struck them, black in black on bright.
Still the stalks loom, mocking all colours' lapse,
askew in rain, look for analogies
and rhymes, like God perhaps, corpse or disease.

Still good for something, as my models right,
because, sawn out against skies whose listless grey
in detail and the whole is blurred,
on them this message, copied word for word:

As wife from husband, briefly wed,
people from country break away.
Harvest was poor, the booty ample.
Oh, the Trustee* has ruined us.
He who beheads the sunflowers, merely suspicious,
will find no witnesses, him the pack will trample.

*Translator's note: The *Treuhand*, a body of government-appointed
receivers whose function was to privatize formerly state-owned property
in the former GDR.

[135]

Allerseelen

Ich flog nach Polen, nahm November mit.
Die Frage, was, wenn polnisch meine Zunge
mir wörtlich wäre und tödlich folgsam beim Ulanenritt –
ich rauchte tief katholisch und auf Lunge –,

blieb wortreich ohne Antwort, deutsch auf deutsch vernarrt:
Zwar schmeichle der Gedanke, sei bizarr, apart,
doch müsse ich bei heimischer Kontrolle
zu Markte tragen meine eingefärbte Wolle.

So nachbarlich durchnäßt, so ferngerückt verloren,
so anverwandt vom Lied und Leid im Lied besessen,
so heimlich zugetan, doch taub auf beiden Ohren,
sind Freunde wir, bis Schmerz, weil nie vergessen
die Narbe (unsre) pocht; umsonst war alles Hoffen:
Die Gräber alle stehn auf Allerseelen offen.

All Souls

I flew to Poland, November at my side.
The question was, if Polish there my tongue
were literal and deadly in obedience when the Ulans ride –
Catholic deep down I smoked, down to the lung –

stayed voluble with no answer, German to German fixed:
The quirk might flatter, because so quaintly mixed.
Yet on returning to the home control
to market I must carry still my dyed-in wool.

So soaked in neighbourliness, so far astray for years,
so much akin to song and grief possessed in song,
so secretly inclined, yet deaf now in both ears,
we're friends till pain, remembered for so long,
the scar (our own) will throb; all hoping was in vain:
All Souls' Day opens each and every grave again.

Sturmwarnung

Im Radio angekündigt, kam von England ein Orkan.
Nur wenig Tote diesmal, überhoch die Schäden
an Sachen, Material, von Klimasorgen nicht zu reden:
Die Stürme könnten, wie der allgemeine Wahn,

sich mehren, bis matt wir sind von einheitlicher Last
und ausgeschlossen wären aus dem Club der Reichen,
denn selbst die D-Mark ließe sich erweichen,
wenn zügelloses Wetter dauerhaft als Gast

hier heimisch wünscht zu werden, wie der Fremden Flut,
die frech, trotz Drogensucht und aidsverseuchtem Blut,
mit uns sich mischen möchte, will uns trüb durchrassen,
so daß wir sie, nicht uns mehr hassen. –
Schon wieder, angekündigt, ein Orkan zuviel,
der keine Grenzen kennt, klopft an und fordert laut Asyl.

Gale Warning

Forecast on radio, from England a hurricane blew.
Not many dead this time, the damage far too great
in things, material, fears for our climate's state:
that gales, like our delusion, general madness, too,

could now increase until, enfeebled by a common load,
we could be dropped and banned from affluence's club
because the D-mark even could receive a rub
if unreined weather for its permanent abode

chose ours, imposed itself, like all that foreign flood
that, brash in drug addiction, AIDS-infected blood,
desires to mix with us, to miscegenate,
so that it's them, no more ourselves, we hate.
And, forecast, yet another most unwelcome such
gate-crashes every frontier, loudmouthed. It's too much.

Vorm ersten Advent

Was teuer wird: das Leben, der Kredit, Benzin!
Im kahlen Garten spärlich Hagebutten glühn.
Auf allgemeinem Grau ein Farbenklecks
erinnert uns an Ehestreit und sommerlichen Sex.

So abgefackelt nach nur bißchen Lustgewinn
krümmt sich Novemberland, bekümmert vom Gebrüll:
kein Penis mehr, doch tausendmal ein Skin
steht für Gewalt und unversorgten Müll.

Der gilt als schlau, der rechnet in Prozenten
den fremden Anteil nach bei deutschen Renten,
als könnte jenen eine Rechnung dienen,
die schweigend grinsen hinter den Gardinen,
wenn draußen Mölln ist, unsre kleine Stadt,
die sich ganz unverhofft ein Fest bereitet hat.

Before the First Sunday in Advent

What's growing costly: living, credit, gasoline!
In the stripped garden sparsely rosehips cast their sheen.
Against the general greyness a few flecks
remind us of our marriage tiffs and summer sex.

So, all burned off, burned out, with little lust thrown in,
Novemberland writhes, by uproar cowed, dejected:
no penis now, but, thousandfold, a skin
stands for new violence, rubbish not collected.

Cunning they think the one who in per cents
works out the foreign share in German pensions,
as though by calculation those could win
who silent behind curtains wait and grin,
when it is Mölln* outside, our little town
that to a quite unhoped-for fête gets down.

*Translator's note: The site of atrocities committed against foreigners
by neo-Nazis in 1992.

Ausser Plan

Auf alte Zeitung, die im Garten treibt, unstetig,
und sich an Dornen reißt, auf Suche nach Ästhetik,
schlägt wütig Gegenwart, ein rüder Hagelschauer;
November spottet aller Schönschrift Dauer.

Schaut nur, die blassen stilgerechten Knaben,
die sich, auf Wunsch, der Stunde Null verschrieben haben.
Jetzt jammern sie, weil selbst auf Stasispitzel
Verlaß nicht ist, um Zeilenschwund und momentanen Kitzel.

Betreten reisen sie, wie altgewohnt, zur nächsten Vernissage,
auf Spesen mürrisch von Premiere zu Premiere
und reden sich bei Billigsekt und Klatsch in Rage;
da kommt Gewalt dem fixen Wortfluß in die Quere
und brüllt aufs neue überlieferten Jargon:
verschreckt (ganz außer Plan) wacht auf das Feuilleton.

Unplanned

On an old daily drifting in the garden, jerkily,
that tears itself on thorns, in search of harmony,
the present, a rude hailstorm, beats thick and fast;
November mocks calligraphy's claim to last.

Just look at any pale, conformist, trendy boy
committed to the zero hour, which gave him joy.
His kind complain, since on no Stasi spy
they can rely now, columns shrink, the thrills run dry.

Sheepish but as of old, to the next vernissage
they travel, their expenses paid, to the next opening night,
with gossip, cheap champagne to fuel the old rage;
but violence breaks up the flow so smooth and bright,
roars out anew a jargon common once as dirt:
alarmed (and quite unplanned), the arts page leaps alert.

Andauernder Regen

Die Angst geht um, November droht zu bleiben.
Nie wieder langer Tage Heiterkeit.
Die letzten Fliegen fallen von den Scheiben,
und Stillstand folgt dem Schnellimbiß der Zeit.

Des Bauherrn Ängste gründen sich auf Fundamente,
denn Pfusch von gestern könnte heut zutage treten,
Die Jugend bangt – schon früh vergreist – um ihre Rente.
Und auch des Volkes Diener üppige Diäten

sind ängstlich rasch verdoppelt worden.
Die Skins mit Schlips und Scheitel kriegen Orden.
Wer dieser Wirtschaft Zukunftsmärkte lobt,
den hat der Zeitgeist regelrecht gedopt,
dem steht Zweidrittelmehrheit stramm, aus Angst geeint;
ein Narr, der im Novemberregen weint.

Persistent Rain

November is here to stay, our fear of it makes plain.
Gone are the long days of unbroken brightness.
The last flies drop from each dull windowpane,
a standstill has replaced time's fast-food lightness.

The property owner's fears are based on real foundations,
since yesterday's botching could come to light today.
Young people – prematurely aged – to pension cares fall prey.
Also, the civil servants' rich remunerations

in anxious haste were doubled by the boards.
Skinheads with ties and partings get awards.
Who praises this economy's market hope
is one the zeitgeist thoroughly could dope,
him a (fear-forged) two-thirds' majority guards in vain;
a fool who'll weep in the November rain.

Die Festung Wächst

Liegt brach das Land zum Fraß der Krähenschar.
Der Maulwurf mehrt sich, und verdächtig häufig
sind längs den Zäunen fremde Hunde läufig.
Wir sollen zahlen: auf die Hand und bar.

Weil in der Mitte liegend, reich und ungeschützt,
hat planend Furcht ein Bauwerk ausgeschwitzt:
als Festung will Novemberland sich sicher machen
vor Roma, Schwarzen, Juden und Fallachen.

Nach Osten hin soll Polen Grenzmark sein;
so schnell fällt nützlich uns Geschichte ein.
Das Burgenbauen war schon immer unsre Lust,
den Wall zu ziehn, die Mauer zu errichten,
und gegen Festungskoller, Stumpfsinn, Lagerfrust
half stets ein Hölderlin im Brotsack mit Gedichten.

The Fortress Grows

The land lies fallow, food now for rooks and crows.
The moles proliferate and, as they'd never done,
suspect, along the fences strange dogs run.
We are to pay: in cash, and through the nose.

Because mid-European, wealthy and vulnerable,
fear sweated out its draughts for a defensive wall:
now as a fortress Novemberland seeks to be
safe from Black, Fellah, Jew, Turk, Romany.

As eastern border Poland will serve again:
so fast we think of history, to our gain.
Building of castles has always been our special joy,
to raise the rampart, excavate the moat;
and against fortress, megrims, dullness, gloom attacks
always a Hölderlin helped with poems in our packs.

Entlaubt

Der Nußbaum leer, hat alles fallenlassen.
Die Körbe schwer, aus schwarzem Schalenbrei
zieh Tinten ich, die Unschuld, die sich weiß beteuert, hassen.
Aus bittrem Sud fließt meine Litanei.

Was wirft hier Blasen, sprengt Beton,
der unsren Parkplatz überm kommunalen Sumpf
so sicher machte? Gehegte Ordnung jeglicher Fasson
ist außer Kurs, und Glieder, ledig, ohne Rumpf,

sind unterwegs, im Gleichschritt wie geübt.
Gestreckte Arme grüßen irgendwas.
Drauf ein Gebrüll, das nur sein Echo liebt,
aus Köpfen, die gedunsen sind vom Haß,
bis daß – Pen, Krach!, welch komisch echter Knall . . .
Komm! Laß uns Nüsse knacken nach dem jüngsten Fall.

Defoliated

The nut tree has dropped all, defoliate.
The baskets heavy, from black husk cellulose
inks I extract that for the innocence professing whiteness
    renders hate.
From bitter broth of pulp my litany flows.

What throws up bubbles, blasts the concrete face
that made our car park over communal bogs
so safe? All sorts of order formerly in place
are out of currency, and trunkless limbs like logs

are on the march, in practised unison.
Extended arms salute a who-knows-what.
Then a great roar that loves its echo alone
from heads all swollen with resentment, hate,
until – bang, crash – a lifelike, laughable pop . . .
Come on! Let's crack some nuts after the latest drop.

Nach kurzer Krankheit

Verschnupft das Land, die Grippe sucht uns heim
und macht aufs Krippenkind sich einen Fieberreim.
Aktive Viren, wach zu neuem Kult,
den wir besänftigt glaubten, pfleglich eingelullt.

Bis uns die Augen triefen und der Blick getrübt,
verrotzt, weil nun auch Taschentücher fehlen,
wird alte Klage jung vertont geübt,
auf daß wir eine Stimme sind beim Hustentropfenzählen.

Kaum ausgeschwitzt, doch noch vom Brüllen heiser,
verhallt Gewalt, bellt leis und auf Verlangen leiser.
Kaum abgeklungen, schrumpft die Grippe zur Legende
und findet in der Talkshow prompt ihr gutes Ende:
ganz locker wird vom Hocker diskutiert,
warum der Mensch sich bei Gelegenheit vertiert.

After Brief Illness

All runny-nosed the land, the flu bug has run wild
and makes itself a rhyme upon the manger child.
Quick viruses, alert to the new cult
we thought assuaged long since, carefully soothed and lulled.

Till our eyes drip, our vision that was blurred
grows snotty too, with hankies scarce in shops,
old moans, set to new music, now are heard,
so that we form one voice while counting cough mixture
    drops.

Hardly yet sweated out, still hoarse with all that roar,
violence fades, barks softly and, if requested, more.
Hardly subsided, the flu shrinks to a legend
and in a talk show finds its happy ending:
quite glibly on their stools now they debate
why on occasion humans lapse from the human state.

Bei klarer Sicht

Komm, Nebel, komm! Und mach uns anonym.
Wir sind ertappt auf frischer (unterlaßner) Tat.
Versalzen welkt nun unser harmloser Salat,
der treuherzig, wie einst Minister Blüm,

mit Gästen rechnete, für die brav andre zahlen.
So lebten wir begünstigt auf Kredit,
doch jemand, der (ein Gott?) am Nebelvorhang zieht,
verriet schon jetzt die Zahlen nächster Wahlen.

Fein rausgeputzt, verkürzt auf Mittelmaß,
der Riß verklebt, der Klassen gröbster Unterschied
bemäntelt. Kein Rüchlein (nein!) erinnerte ans Gas,
und nur die dritte Strophe galt (halbblau) im Lied.
Auf Siegers Seite lebten wir, behütet und getrennt,
bis uns die Einheit schlug, die keine Gnade kennt.

In Clear Perspective

Come, fog, o come! Make us anonymous.
We have been caught red-handed in the (undone) act.
Our salad wilts with too much of the salt it lacked,
as guileless as once Blüm, our Minister, was,

expecting guests that others pay for, raising no objections.
We lived on credit, privileged and certain,
but somebody (a God?) who lifts the long fog's curtain
has leaked the figures for the next elections.

Dressed up, all shortened to the medium size,
tears plastered over, class differences most crass
all cloaked. No whiff (oh no!) reminded them of gas.
The anthem's third stanza only valid (hummed with lowered
    eyes).
On the victor's side we lived, divided, safe from stress,
till unity struck us and proved merciless.

Wer kommt?

Novemberschwärze vor verwaschnem Hell:
die letzten Sonnenblumen stehen schwarz Modell.
Seitab verglühen restlich Hagebutten.
Weil oben ohne, nässen Bäume ohne Kutten

gestaffelt und vereinzelt, auch der Nußbaum leer.
Fern übt mit Waffenschein ein einsames Gewehr.
Den häßlich kleinen Unterschied vertuscht der Nebel.
Ach, wüßt ich dem Adventsgebrüll doch einen Knebel.

Wer kommt, ist da, multipliziert?
Im Radio angekündigt, nur wie üblich, ein Orkan,
der seine Wut gewöhnlich unterwegs verliert.
Vor jähem Frost geschützt der blanke Wasserhahn,
verschnürt die Päckchen, fertig zum Versand;
demnächst droht Weihnacht dem Novemberland.

Who's Coming?

November blackness against bright tints effete:
as models the last sunflowers blackly sit.
Beside them the residual rosehips fade.
Bare at the tops, trees, cowl-less, drip and shed

what's left, in groups or single, even the nut tree bare.
A lonely gun that's licensed rehearses from afar.
Fog blots and blurs the ugly little doubt.
I wish I knew a gag, too, for the advent shout.

Who's coming, is here, and multiplied?
As usual the radio forecasts a mere hurricane
that usually on the way loses its force and stride.
The water tap's been lagged against sudden frost again,
the parcels are tied up, ready for mailing; and
imminent Christmas threatens our Novemberland.